What readers are saying about
Scripted GUI Testing with Ruby

If you care about your application, you care about testing. And if you
have an application with a user interface, you should care about testing it. This book gives you what you need to start testing in an agile
manner, using a modern programming language and excellent techniques. This book covers a wide range of GUI testing and should be in
every developer's bookshelf.

► **Ola Bini**
JRuby Core Developer, ThoughtWorks

This book provides the most thorough and enjoyable introduction
to GUI testing in Ruby (or any language, for that matter) I've yet to
encounter. It was not only technically enlightening but a pleasure to
read—something few technical books achieve. I am tempted to buy
copies for every QA tester I know—and probably a lot of developers,
too!

► **Thomas Lockney**
Software Developer

Ian Dees brings the joy of Ruby to the task of GUI testing, allowing
you to "let the computers and the people each do what they're good
at." Testers and nontesters alike will find value in his discussions of
automating GUI actions to both save time and improve quality.

► **David Mullet**
The Ruby on Windows blog

Scripted GUI Testing with Ruby is a must-read for small to medium-sized development shops building any kind of GUI application. Although aimed at the QA segment, the book's readability and well-considered refactorings will be a benefit to developers. More important, by providing a concrete soup-to-nuts introduction to RSpec, it shows a path bridging that crucial gap between product designers and implementors. Ian shows us that a QA's job—long-considered monotonous and akin to visiting the dentist—can in fact bring clarity of understanding to all members of a project. And even better, time and money that would have been wasted on manual click-and-pray testing can now be dedicated to truly creative software destruction, leaving the boring bits to the robots. For that reason alone, QAs, developers, and project managers need to pick up this book so they can understand what QA and communication are really about.

► **Duncan Beevers**
  Developer, Kongregate

Scripted GUI Testing with Ruby really is unique in the market, and I'm glad to see it published. Like Ian, I wish I'd had this in my hands four years ago. After reading and working through *Scripted GUI Testing with Ruby*, I have several new toolsets in my testing arsenal. I had heard a bit about some of the tools Ian covers in this book, but now I know how they'll apply to my work and, thanks to the examples, exactly how to use them.

► **Alex LeDonne**
  Senior Software Quality Analyst

Scripted GUI Testing with Ruby

Scripted GUI Testing with Ruby

Ian Dees

The Pragmatic Bookshelf
Raleigh, North Carolina   Dallas, Texas

Many of the designations used by manufacturers and sellers to distinguish their products are claimed as trademarks. Where those designations appear in this book, and The Pragmatic Programmers, LLC was aware of a trademark claim, the designations have been printed in initial capital letters or in all capitals. The Pragmatic Starter Kit, The Pragmatic Programmer, Pragmatic Programming, Pragmatic Bookshelf and the linking *g* device are trademarks of The Pragmatic Programmers, LLC.

Every precaution was taken in the preparation of this book. However, the publisher assumes no responsibility for errors or omissions, or for damages that may result from the use of information (including program listings) contained herein.

Our Pragmatic courses, workshops, and other products can help you and your team create better software and have more fun. For more information, as well as the latest Pragmatic titles, please visit us at

> http://www.pragprog.com

ISBN-10: 1-934356-18-2

ISBN-13: 978-1-9343561-8-0

Printed on acid-free paper.

P1.0 printing, July 2008

Version: 2008-7-15

Contents

Chapter 1

Introduction

What do you want from your tests?

Your answer to that question will shape your software testing efforts to a great degree. It will especially affect how you do your GUI tests and in particular what role automation plays for you.

Lots of folks talk about automated testing, but the term is a bit of a misnomer. All but the most deluded toolkit vendors admit that testing requires human ingenuity. So, the whole "manual vs. automated" argument is a bit of a red herring.

There are tasks that computers are good at, such as generating a million-word document on the fly to try to crash a spell checker. And there are things only a human tester will catch, such as when something doesn't look *quite* right about a particular layout in landscape mode.

So, why not let the computers and the people each do what they're good at doing? Really, all testing is human activity. Some tasks are just more computer-assisted than others, which is why I prefer the term *scripted testing* over the more traditional *automated testing*.

In this book, we'll look at ways that writing test scripts can make you a better tester. We'll cast our net both deep and wide. In the first half of this book, we'll delve deeply into a real-world app and come up with a set of Ruby scripts that exercise all of its features. In the second half, we'll take a broader survey of GUI testing topics.

1.1 Testing for Fun and Profit

Back to our original question: what do you want from your tests?

Most answers to that question boil down to "fun" or "profit." Take, for instance, this quote:

Testing is the process of executing a program with the intent of finding errors.[1]

This is clearly in the "profit" category. How much testing can we afford to do, and how much money will we save by catching bugs before they get out the door? Actuaries have tables of industry-wide numbers on this topic, and every other testing book seems to open with the same stats on how many bajillion dollars we're losing this year.

How about this one?

The purpose of testing is to make quality visible.[2]

This one is more about the "fun" side: shining a light into the darkness, making the invisible spring forth. So artistic!

I can already hear the battle lines being drawn. Before anyone gets hurt, let's talk about a Grand Unified Theory of sorts between the two camps.

What We're Looking For

Let's look at the "profit" answer for a second. If the purpose of testing is to find bugs, what kinds of bugs are we looking for?

The act of *running* an automated script—especially a GUI one—may find regressions, but it isn't likely to find old bugs. After all, a simple script will typically do the same thing each time (although in Chapter 7, *Keep 'Em Guessing: Introducing Randomness*, on page 89, we're going to see some exceptions). If it didn't unearth that botched search on the first run, it's probably not going to after the tenth.

On the other hand, *writing* a script can find some of the earliest problems to be introduced: bad or missing requirements.

An example is in order here. Imagine a word processor's Undo feature. The UI designer has dutifully spelled out what kinds of actions can be undone, how the menu item changes its name to Undo Typing or Undo Delete or whatever, and so on.

---

1. *The Art of Software Testing* [Mye79]
2. *The Complete Guide to Software Testing* [Het84]

But one thing that no one thought of—or rather, everyone thought of differently—is what happens when someone undoes *all* his changes and then exits the program. Should the word processor prompt him to save?[3] The UI design seems to say so: all modified documents should be saved.

So in our hypothetical example, that's how the programmer implemented the feature. Any change, including Undo, sets a "dirty" flag somewhere, which the app checks at exit time. But that's not how the tester wrote the script:

```
type_in "Hello"
undo
fail "Undo failed to delete 'Hello'" unless document.empty?
exit :expect_prompt => false
```

The tester interpreted the design as having a loophole for empty documents, in contrast to the programmer's more literal view. They flag down the designer, and the three of them sit down to hash things out.

An interesting thing happened here. The tests became the centerpiece of a conversation—between designer, developer, and tester. And we've landed firmly in the warm and fuzzy "shine a light on quality" aspect of the "fun" motive.

Caveat Tester

Before we get too carried away, it's worth noting that there is a cost to automation. It will almost certainly take longer to write a program that clicks a button than just to click the button yourself and see what happens. And test scripts can watch only what they're told to watch; your judgment is vastly more discerning.

In other words, automation is *never* a replacement for manual activity. Use it to extend your reach—to do things you couldn't have done with your bare hands.

For instance, use automation to tell you a few moments after someone's check-in whether the changes are good enough to spend time testing by hand.[4] Or have the build run all night with millions of different input combinations. Or script a complicated setup activity so that you can quickly and repeatably demonstrate a bug you found manually.

---

3. Of course, the tester will be asking lots of other questions, too, such as "Will the program hang or crash if the list of undone changes has 10,000 actions it?"

4. http://www.martinfowler.com/articles/continuousIntegration.html

Also, please consider that some domains are better suited than others for automation. Test oracles—pass/fail criteria—are much easier to write for text than for, say, audio or complicated images.

1.2 Behavior-Driven Development and RSpec

The idea of tests as conversation pieces isn't a new one. You're no doubt familiar with the idea of *test-driven development*, or TDD, whose practitioners write their code-level unit tests before doing anything else.

When TDD was a new buzzword, skeptics heard that these enthusiasts were touting their tests as proof that their programs worked. But unit tests aren't written that way—an algorithm that works in a couple of specific cases might fail in a thousand other cases. Critics were absolutely right to be suspicious of these kinds of claims.

The important idea in TDD *wasn't* the tests; it was the fact that writing the tests forces developers to think through how their code will behave. People tried renaming the practice to test-driven *design*, but of course everyone still got hung up on that first word.

What people were calling *tests* were really *examples* of how a piece of code was supposed to behave. So, the successors to TDD had names like *example-driven development* or *behavior-driven development*.

From Tests to Behavior

It may seem surprising that people fretted so much about what to name their practice. But "getting the words right" is one of the key ideas behind BDD. If the tests are going to be a lingua franca among the programmers, testers, and users, then it had better be a clear language.

In the earliest days of BDD, proponents focused on object-level unit tests. Even within the narrow scope of individual source code files, developers found it helpful to write their examples in a format that they could credibly show to a subject-matter expert and say, "Is this right?"

Of course, end users don't care that your AbstractFactoryPattern class works; they care whether the *program* works. Fortunately, the ideas behind BDD apply at the application level, too. Instead of describing source code, you're describing a GUI. Rather than giving examples in a programming language, you're giving them in a natural language. But you're still focusing on writing something that your customers (or someone who understands their needs) can read or perhaps even modify.

RSpec's Roles

RSpec was the first Ruby implementation of the ideas behind BDD and followed its early focus on source code. Tests—referred to as *examples*—were written in Ruby and typically exercised individual methods of a class. For instance, here's how the developer of a Stereo class might test its mute() method:

```
describe 'The mute button' do
  it 'reduces the volume to zero' do
    @stereo.volume = 10
    @stereo.mute
    @stereo.volume.should == 0
  end
end
```

As you can see, example notation is a bit technical, but it's still legible. It doesn't take a Ruby expert to figure out what the test does. You could imagine the developer huddling around a printout with the team's resident audiophile to figure out another facet of the object's behavior, such as whether the unmute feature should be instant or gradual.

As nice as RSpec examples are for describing individual features, there are clearer ways to describe application behavior as a whole. The Story Runner, a recent addition to RSpec, reads and runs tests that are written in plain English.

For example, if your team is trying to figure out how your word processor should create new documents on your lab's French-localized machine, you and the designers and coders might come up with something like this:

```
Given a North American locale
When I open a new word processor document
Then the paper size should be "Letter"

Given a European locale
When I open a new word processor document
Then the paper size should be "A4"
```

It's wordy but clear. It's also *running code*, which RSpec's Story Runner can execute on a thousand different combinations of locale and operating system.

And it can run it all over again in six months, when the next version comes out with the development team's new localization code.

Which Notation to Use

Many projects use both flavors of RSpec: Ruby examples for unit tests and plain-English stories for UI tests. Of course, your program doesn't have to be written in Ruby for you to benefit from RSpec. Although you'll write your unit tests in your app's language, you can still test the user interface with RSpec.

In this book, we're going to start from the ground up, and that means we'll see the Ruby side of RSpec first—because "classic" RSpec example notation is *the* way to test Ruby libraries like the one we'll build. The plain-English Story Runner format will pop up later, when we talk about the role of tests in program design.

For the many facets of RSpec that aren't addressed here, you may want to refer to the numerous examples and article links on the documentation page of RSpec's website.[5]

1.3 About This Book

As much as I love talking about GUI tests, it's much more illustrative to *show* them. So, we're going to spend the first half of this book building up a test script ("test" in the sense of "set of examples") for a live application. I don't mean some toy "pet store" sample project; I mean a real program people are using for something other than writing books on testing.

By the halfway point, we'll have a somewhat typical GUI test project on our hands, with the same refactoring and changing of direction you'd see in the real world. From there, we'll branch out into a survey of GUI testing topics, leaving behind our one big example for several smaller illustrations.

Who It's For

This book is for testers who code and for coders who test. It's the book I wish I had four years ago. That's when I faced the equally unpleasant tasks of fixing old, broken GUI tests and coaxing a rickety third-party

---

5. See http://rspec.info/documentation/.

toolkit into running new tests. I started looking for a how-to guide on GUI testing to help me down this road.

Unfortunately, there were none. Plenty of people had written beautifully about testing in general but not about user interfaces specifically. What few GUI books did exist were long, dry, restricted to technologies I couldn't use, or built on test frameworks that looked like someone's homework assignment.

A lot of folks are having the same problem I had. Some of you are testers who are sick of hearing the "testers don't code" slander and want to use scripting in your palette of techniques. Others are QA engineers tired of the messy generated code and clunky APIs of GUI toolkits. Still others are software developers who want to test and improve their own programs.

How to Use It

The best way to get a feel for GUI test scripts is to write a bunch of 'em. You'll get the most out of the examples by following along and typing in the code yourself. If you want to compare your code with the version in the book, the latter is available at http://www.pragprog.com/titles/idgtr/source_code.

If you're a web tester, you may want to peek ahead at Chapter 9, *Testing the Tubes: Web Applications*, on page 115, where we deal with concerns specific to web apps. Then come back and read Part I—although it uses a desktop app for its examples, you'll find a lot of practices there that are relevant for testing of any kind.

The code examples in this book are written in Ruby. That is how we are going to create the building blocks to support those plainspoken English-like tests. You don't have to be a Ruby expert to follow along, but you should probably have some basic familiarity with the language. We'll be writing short programs, installing libraries, running scripts from the command line, and so on.

Regulars from other scripting languages can pick up most of the Ruby they need from the online version of the Pickaxe book.[6] If, on the other hand, this is your first scripting project, you may want to read Brian Marick's *Everyday Scripting with Ruby* [Mar06].

---

6. http://www.ruby-doc.org/docs/ProgrammingRuby

About the Examples

This book follows several conventions that are common among Ruby programs. If you've written a lot of Ruby, you've probably used most of these, but if you're new to the language, most of them are less than obvious.

Implicit return: Since Ruby can use a function's last expression as the return value, I will usually omit return statements unless one is needed for clarity.

Ternary operator: Simple assignments will often use a ? b : c as shorthand for if a then b else c; end.

Logical assignments: Ruby programmers frequently use a ||= b (an abbreviation of a = a || b) to say, "If a doesn't already have a value, make it equal to b." A related, but less common, shortcut is a &&= b in place of a = a && b.

method_missing(): Ruby's method_missing() hook lets you specify what to do when a nonexistent function is called. This feature can be abused, so I use it only in a couple of cases—mainly when an object needs to support a potentially infinite set of method names.

Several examples involve typing text into a command prompt. I'll adopt whichever format is most appropriate for each example (C:\> for Windows, $ for others). In practice, they're mostly interchangeable—sometimes with minor tweaks, such as dropping the word sudo if you're on Windows.

1.4 Acknowledgments

I'm indebted to a great many people for their indulgence and help on this book. Many thanks to Jackie Carter, my awesome editor, for patiently shepherding this undertaking and for her constant attention to flow; my lovely family for putting up with a rambling, distracted me for over a year; Ola Bini for always finding a better way to say it in Ruby; James Bach for injecting a healthy dose of reality; Duncan Beevers, Alex LeDonne, Thomas Lockney, and David Mullet for making sure the darn thing *works*; Ryan Davis for ZenTest subtleties; Daniel Steinberg and the Prags for rolling the dice on this project; Brian Marick for writing the book that inspired mine; David Chelimsky and the RSpec crew for setting the standard for clear test language; and of course Matz for optimizing Ruby for programmer happiness.

Part I

One Big Example

*I'm an idealist. I don't know where I'm going, but I'm on my
way.*
  ▶ Carl Sandburg

Chapter 2

An Early Success

You have read the disclaimers. You're undertaking your automation
project with open eyes. Your application domain is well-suited for
scripted testing. Now what?

We're going to spend the next few chapters building an automated test
suite from the ground up. Along the way, we'll look for ways to streamline our tests and make our scripts easier to understand.

In this chapter, we're going to familiarize ourselves with the tools we
need and write a simple GUI control script. We'll leave the writing of
pass/fail tests for later chapters. For now, it'll be enough to get confident with the basics: simulating keystrokes, pushing buttons, and so
on.

2.1 First Steps

Rather than collecting a bunch of toy examples, we'll choose a single
real-world program and exercise its user interface thoroughly over the
course of the book. Before we plunge into the craft of test writing, let's
get an early success into the logbook. We'll create a basic but working
automation script and start controlling a live application.

Some of the code in this chapter is a bit dense. We're working toward
writing self-descriptive code like this:

```
note.select_all
note.cut
note.text.should == ''
```

But to get there, we need to do a little plumbing work. You'll see repetitive sections and hairy API calls in the coming pages that just scream

to be distilled into something cleaner. Keep in mind the places you'd want to tidy up; we'll likely get to them in future chapters.

Choose Your Own Adventure

As you follow along in the examples, you'll be able to choose which platform to implement them on. Door #1 is the Windows door, through which you'll see classic Win32 API calls driving an application. Door #2 is the cross-platform door. Behind it, you'll test a Swing app on the Java runtime using JRuby.[1] The screenshots from Door #2 came from a Mac, but the examples should work almost anywhere Java runs, including Linux or Windows (but probably not Java-powered toasters).

The Windows-specific sections will usually be a few pages longer than the corresponding cross-platform ones. Am I hiding a bunch of extra secrets there? No—it's just that the two tracks begin at two different places.

For Java, we are coming out of the blocks with a full-blown GUI automation library from the good folks at NetBeans. But the Ruby GUI test options for Windows are a little less mature, so we are going to build our own.

The two tracks will eventually converge as we find concepts that are common to both worlds. Until then, I'll mark the parts that are specific to one or the other. Feel free to read either or both—they don't depend on each other.

Chosen your platform yet? Good! Now, let's find an application to subject to our scripting ambitions.

Finding a Guinea Pig

What program should we test? Without a doubt, you have your own GUI projects you want to automate. It would be nice if the examples in this book addressed the same kinds of challenges you encounter in the real world, so we'll write a test script for an app that real customers have been using in the wild.

Keep in mind that the values we'll be stressing—clear test scripts and reasonable expectations of automation—will serve *any* project well. We could base a book's worth of test scripts around a Windows GUI, a web application, a Unix console program, or what have you.

---

1. A Ruby implementation written in Java.

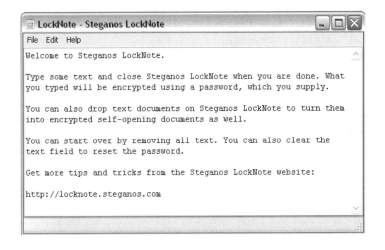

Figure 2.1: LOCKNOTE'S MAIN WINDOW

But let's "stack the deck" a bit by choosing an application that fits the format of this book well. We'd like something simple so that we can write some meaningful tests for it in four chapters. That probably means a text-based app, since comparing images is a huge topic in its own right.

Meet LockNote...

A bit of searching on SourceForge turns up LockNote, a Notepad-like text editor for Windows that encrypts your files when you save them.[2] A screenshot of LockNote's main window appears in Figure 2.1.

LockNote will serve our needs amply. It is available for free, so you can follow along with the examples in this book. It serves a well-defined, readily understood purpose. It uses standard Windows components such as edit controls, push buttons, and check boxes. Finally, its focus on text means that the techniques we use for testing Undo, Find/Replace, and Cut/Copy/Paste will be easy to apply to other projects.

So if you're following along in Windows, grab LockNote's "source + binary" distribution from the release page.[3] Why do we need LockNote's

---

2. http://sf.net/projects/locknote—I have nothing to do with LockNote or the Steganos company, by the way.

3. http://downloads.sf.net/locknote/locknote-1.0.3-src%2Bbinary.zip

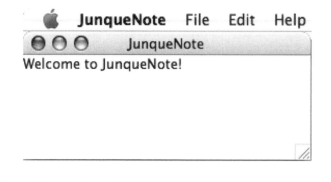

Figure 2.2: JUNQUENOTE'S MAIN WINDOW

source code? It's in C++, and isn't this is a *Ruby* book? Yes, but one small piece of that source will come in handy later.

...and JunqueNote

LockNote will do just fine for Windows testing, but what about the cross-platform track? For that, I've written a simple clone of LockNote called JunqueNote (see Figure 2.2). Its encryption is not beefy enough to use on real data, but it's feature-for-feature compatible with LockNote.

JunqueNote runs on the Java runtime, but like the tests you'll be writing, its source code (which comes with this book) is in Ruby. To use it, you'll need to download and install JRuby.[4]

You'll also need to install the Cheri gem for drawing JunqueNote's UI, as well as the Crypt gem for encrypting the saved files. If the jruby executable is in your PATH, the following two commands will do the trick:

```
$ sudo jruby -S gem install cheri
$ sudo jruby -S gem install crypt
```

Now, you should be able to start JunqueNote by grabbing a copy of junquenote_app.rb and running the following command:[5]

```
$ jruby junquenote_app.rb
```

---

4. http://jruby.codehaus.org
5. http://www.pragprog.com/titles/idgtr/source_code/junquenote/junquenote_app.rb

Take a Test-Drive

In the upcoming chapters, we're going to exercise every menu command, dialog box, and keyboard shortcut in LockNote and JunqueNote. But for now, let's just focus on getting the software running and poking a couple of buttons using Ruby.

We're going to start with the simplest code that could possibly work. That means using a few platform-specific calls at first, and these are naturally going to differ between the two apps. But we'll eventually be able to test both programs from the same script.

In the meantime, take a few minutes to explore LockNote or JunqueNote by hand. Create a couple of password-protected documents. Type in your impressions of this book so far (don't worry, I can't read them: they're encrypted!). Experiment with edge cases such as entering a mismatched password/confirmation pair or hitting Undo when you haven't changed anything. I'll wait here for you.

Ready to move on? Great! The next section introduces the Windows-specific calls you'll need to drive LockNote. A few pages later, we'll cover the cross-platform JunqueNote app in Section 2.3, *Door #2: Swing with JRuby*, on page 22.

2.2 Door #1: Windows

I'm all for jumping right in, but our first couple of techniques merit a bit of discussion before we try them for real.

Launching the App

First up—the following Ruby code will start almost any program:

```
system 'C:\Path\To\Program.exe'
```

But Ruby will pause indefinitely at that line, sitting patiently until someone manually closes the program—not very conducive to automated testing! To return control to Ruby right away, we'll pair system() with Windows' start command (and switch to forward slashes for quoting reasons):

```
system 'start "" "C:/Path/To/Program.exe"'
```

This line will tell Windows to launch the app, but it doesn't tell us much about the results. Did the program start successfully? Did it crash? Did we try to run a nonexistent program? To answer these questions and to gain control of the app, we'll need to find its main window using some platform-specific mojo.

Finding the Main Window

Ruby can call Windows functions nearly as easily as regular Ruby class methods, thanks to the Win32API library that ships with the Ruby one-click installer for Windows.[6] A Win32API object is a lot like a plain ol' Ruby Proc.[7] It supplies us with a call() method to invoke its assigned Windows function.

For this step, we'll need the FindWindow() API call to search for the program's main window by title. To bridge the gap between the dynamically typed Ruby world and Windows's static C types, Ruby needs hints at the parameter types. First, let's look at the C function signature for FindWindow():

```
HWND FindWindow(LPCTSTR windowClass, LPCTSTR title);
```

So, FindWindow() needs two string parameters:

- The *window class*, which allows us to narrow our search to a specific kind of window, such as a button or edit control. Since we're just searching for a plain ol' window, we're going to pass in a NULL pointer, which we do by using Ruby's nil identifier.

- The window's title.

In the shorthand of Ruby's Win32API library, the (LPCTSTR, LPCTSTR) function signature shown earlier is abbreviated to ['P', 'P']. Each 'P' denotes a string pointer argument.

FindWindow() returns an HWND, or *window handle*, which is the unique number assigned to this window. We'll use that number to take control of the program. Ruby needs a hint for this return value. Again, we use a shorthand notation: 'L' for "long integer."

The complete Ruby declaration for FindWindow() looks like this:

```
find_window = Win32API.new 'user32', 'FindWindow', ['P', 'P'], 'L'
```

And we use it like so:

```
handle = find_window.call nil, 'Window Title'
```

---

6. http://rubyforge.org/frs/?group_id=167. The examples in this book were written using Ruby 1.8.6.
7. http://www.ruby-doc.org/core/classes/Proc.html

There's a bit more to it, of course. A program typically takes a couple of seconds to launch completely and display its main window. If we call FindWindow() the instant we start our app, the answer will come back zero, meaning "no such window." We'll eventually wrap the function in a while loop to keep calling it until we get a nonzero answer.

A Working Test Script

Now we know how to launch a Windows program from Ruby and how to find a running application. It's time to put those two pieces together into one script.

Save the following code on your hard drive as windows_basics.rb. I've got LockNote installed in C:\LockNote; you'll need to adjust the script if your copy is in a differently named folder.

```
early_success/windows_basics.rb
require 'Win32API'

❶ def user32(name, param_types, return_value)
    Win32API.new 'user32', name, param_types, return_value
  end

find_window = user32 'FindWindow', ['P', 'P'], 'L'

system 'start "" "C:/LockNote/LockNote.exe"'

  sleep 0.2 while (main_window = find_window.call \
❷   nil, 'LockNote - Steganos LockNote') <= 0

puts "The main window's handle is #{main_window}."
```

As we prepare the script, let's look at a couple of points of interest in the code.

Since every Win32 call in this book comes from user32.dll, we've defined a helper function at ❶ to avoid having to type Win32API.new 'user32', ... every time. At ❷, we use a nonobvious feature of Ruby variable scoping: main_window retains its value, even after the while loop exits.

Go ahead and run what you have so far:

```
C:\> ruby windows_basics.rb
```

If all goes well, you'll see LockNote launch, and the console will print a nonzero number identifying the program's main window. Exit the program manually—we'll find a way to close it from our script later in this chapter.

Now that we've created a basic script that launches an application, let's add a few features to actually *control* the program.

Typing Text

Simulated typing of text is something we're going to add in several stages. For now, we're just going to type lowercase letters and spaces. We'll add mixed case and punctuation (things that require key combinations) as we need them.

As we did with FindWindow(), let's start with the C definition of the Windows keybd_event() function:

```
void keybd_event(
  BYTE keyCode,
  BYTE unused,
  DWORD event,
  DWORD extraInfo);
```

For now, we need to worry only about the keyCode and event parameters. They specify which key on the keyboard we're referring to and whether we're simulating the key going up or down.

The BYTE and DWORD parameter types are, respectively, 8-bit characters and long integers, or 'I' and 'L' in Ruby-speak. The function doesn't return a value, so we give it a 'V' for void.

We'll need a couple of Windows-specific constants representing the "up" and "down" events, too. Add this code to the end of your script:

early_success/windows_basics.rb

```
keybd_event = user32 'keybd_event', ['I', 'I', 'L', 'L'], 'V'

KEYEVENTF_KEYDOWN = 0
KEYEVENTF_KEYUP = 2
```

Now, we'll teach our script to type in a few words. On its own, keybd_event() doesn't support the notion of capital or lowercase letters; it deals in keystrokes. In other words, pressing the A key looks the same to keybd_event(), whether Caps Lock is on or off.

Many of the "virtual key codes" required by keybd_event() are cryptically assigned numbers, but at least the basics are easy. Whether we're typing capital or lowercase letters, the alphabetic keys are always represented by the ASCII codes for capital letters *A–Z*—and hence the call to upcase() at ❶.

early_success/windows_basics.rb

```
❶  "this is some text".upcase.each_byte do |b|
     keybd_event.call b, 0, KEYEVENTF_KEYDOWN, 0
     sleep 0.05
     keybd_event.call b, 0, KEYEVENTF_KEYUP, 0
     sleep 0.05
   end
```

Go ahead and add the previous section to the end of your script and then run it again. Did you get the sensation of watching over someone's shoulder as they type? Excellent. Exit LockNote (you can answer "No" to the save prompt for now), and I'll meet you in the next section. For extra credit, you can rerun the script with Caps Lock on and see how the same *keystrokes* can generate different *characters*.

Exiting the App

Until now, you've been closing LockNote manually after each run of the script. Let's look at a way to automate that process a little.

A Close Call

We'll need a new Windows API call to send the Close command to LockNote:

```
BOOL PostMessage(
    HWND window,
    UINT message,
    WPARAM wParam,
    LPARAM lParam);
```

PostMessage() sends an event to a window. As we discussed earlier, the window is identified by its integer handle, or HWND. The message has its own unique integer ID, plus two parameters, also integers. The function returns a BOOL, yet another integer type. Four integer parameters, returning an integer—this one is going to be easy to translate to Ruby.

The way we tell a program that someone has clicked its Close button is to send it the WM_SYSCOMMAND message with the first parameter set to SC_CLOSE (the second parameter is unused this time). The numeric values of this message and its parameter are defined by Microsoft; we'll just hard-code them here.

\\// **Joe Asks...**

What Do We Need Control IDs For?

Each window has a unique window handle. So, why are we introducing a new "control ID" concept?

The difference is that a window handle is assigned by Windows when the window is *created*, whereas a control ID is assigned by the developer when the program is *written*. The No button in a dialog box will have a different window handle every time the program runs, but it will always have a control ID of 7.

Add this code to the end of your script:

early_success/windows_basics.rb

```
post_message = user32 'PostMessage', ['L', 'L', 'L', 'L'], 'L'

WM_SYSCOMMAND = 0x0112
SC_CLOSE = 0xF060

post_message.call main_window, WM_SYSCOMMAND, SC_CLOSE, 0
```

When you run the new version of the script, the app should now exit on its own. Well, almost. Since we've typed text into the window and then tried to exit, we're now staring at a save prompt. And we'll need another trick in our toolkit to deal with that.

The No Button

There are lots of ways to say "No" to a dialog box. We can press Alt+N. In some dialog boxes, we can press Esc. But both those approaches are keyboard-based, and we already know how to press keys from Ruby. Let's teach our script to use the mouse instead.

We want to click the No button inside that save dialog box. To find an item inside a dialog box, we'll use the GetDlgItem() function:

```
HWND GetDlgItem(HWND dialog, int control);
```

The control parameter is the No button's control ID, defined by Microsoft to be IDNO, or 7.

Add this code to the end of your script:

`early_success/windows_basics.rb`

```
get_dlg_item = user32 'GetDlgItem', ['L', 'L'], 'L'
```

❶
❷
```
dialog = timeout(3) do
  sleep 0.2 while (h = find_window.call \
    nil, 'Steganos LockNote') <= 0; h
end

IDNO = 7
button = get_dlg_item.call dialog, IDNO
```

The block of code at ❷, where we find the save prompt by its window title, looks very similar to the way we found the main window in Section 2.2, *A Working Test Script*, on page 17.

The only difference is at ❶, where we call timeout() to bail out of the loop if it takes too long. Other than that, it kind of feels like we're repeating ourselves. Hold that thought—we'll return to it in a later chapter.

Once we've found the No button, we need to get the coordinates of its upper-left and lower-right corners. The GetWindowRect() API call gives us all four of these values in one C structure:

```
BOOL GetWindowRect(HWND window, LPRECT rectangle);
```

A RECT contains four integers laid out one after the other in memory. The only way to have any control over memory placement with Ruby is inside a string, so we'll need to pack() these four values into a string to pass into the function and then unpack() them when we're done. The notation is similar to the one we used for Win32API's parameter types. To prepare four integer coordinates for Windows to fill in, we'd say [0, 0, 0, 0].pack 'LLLL'.

Add the following code to your script:

`early_success/windows_basics.rb`

```
get_window_rect = user32 'GetWindowRect', ['L', 'P'], 'I'

rectangle = [0, 0, 0, 0].pack 'L*'
get_window_rect.call button, rectangle
left, top, right, bottom = rectangle.unpack 'L*'
```

❶
```
puts "The No button is #{right - left} pixels wide."
```

Since we haven't added the code to click the mouse button yet, how do we know the call to GetWindowRect() worked? For now, we'll just throw in a debugging statement at ❶ to tell us the width of the No button. Go ahead and run the script. Does the reported width value look sensible? On a typical Windows setup, it should be 75 pixels or so.

Clicking the Button

Now, we can actually click the button. First, we call SetCursorPos() to move the mouse over the button; then, we call mouse_event() twice to simulate a left click (which consists of two events: the left button goes down and then back up).

SetCursorPos() takes two integer parameters representing the mouse's X and Y coordinates. mouse_event() takes five integers, but we'll be using only the first parameter, which indicates what the mouse is doing—left button up, right button down, and so forth. We've already seen how to translate simple functions like these into Ruby, so let's gloss over the C function definitions and go right to our script. Add the following code:

early_success/windows_basics.rb

```
set_cursor_pos = user32 'SetCursorPos', ['L', 'L'], 'I'

mouse_event = user32 'mouse_event', ['L', 'L', 'L', 'L', 'L'], 'V'

MOUSEEVENTF_LEFTDOWN = 0x0002
MOUSEEVENTF_LEFTUP = 0x0004

center = [(left + right) / 2, (top + bottom) / 2]

❶ set_cursor_pos.call *center

mouse_event.call MOUSEEVENTF_LEFTDOWN, 0, 0, 0, 0
mouse_event.call MOUSEEVENTF_LEFTUP, 0, 0, 0, 0
```

Don't miss the familiar parameter-expansion asterisk at ❶ to expand the center array into two parameters.

Close any open copies of LockNote and run the script again. This time, the mouse click should land right in the middle of the No button at the end.

And that's a great stopping point for the Windows code for now.

2.3 Door #2: Swing with JRuby

Welcome to the cross-platform path, where we'll test the JunqueNote application on the Java runtime, with help from the JRuby interpreter.

Apps Are Objects

Launching an app is simple in JRuby. Both our test script and JunqueNote will be running in the same Java virtual machine. The script assumes that the implementation of JunqueNote lives inside the JunqueNoteApp class. This class could have been written in *any* language that targets the Java runtime: Java, Groovy, JRuby, Jython, and so on.[8]

All you have to do is use the same syntax you'd use to create any Ruby object:

```
JunqueNoteApp.new
```

That'll eventually bring up the main window, but it'll take a few seconds. Before we can use this code in a real script, we'll need to account for the delay.

Pushing the Swing with Jemmy

To manipulate JunqueNote's windows and controls, we're going to turn to Jemmy, an open source library that can drive Java user interfaces built on the Swing library.[9] Jemmy is written in Java, but it works transparently in JRuby.

For each Swing class representing a type of GUI control—such as JButton, JTextField, or JMenuBar—Jemmy provides an "operator" to drive that control—JButtonOperator, JTextFieldOperator, or JMenuBarOperator.

JunqueNote's main window is a JFrame, so we can search for it using a JFrameOperator:

```
require 'java'
require 'jemmy.jar'
```

❶ `include_class 'org.netbeans.jemmy.operators.JFrameOperator'`

❷ `main_window = JFrameOperator.new 'JunqueNote'`

As long as jemmy.jar is somewhere in JRuby's load path, we can require it like we would a regular Ruby library. From that point on, Jemmy classes are available in Ruby under their fully spelled-out Java names, like org.netbeans.jemmy.operators.JFrameOperator.

---

8. It happens to be written in JRuby. See code/junquenote/junquenote_app.rb for details.
9. http://jemmy.netbeans.org

But we'd like to be able to say just JFrameOperator, without all that org.netbeans stuff before it. The include_class call at ❶ sets up this easier-to-type alias for us.

The call at ❷ will block until the main window appears. Later, we'll adjust Jemmy's timeouts so that we won't be drumming our fingers for ages if something has gone wrong.

OK, enough talk. Ready to try this stuff out for real?

Make It So

Turning our burgeoning knowledge of JRuby into a working script is as simple as combining our app-launching code with a Jemmy operator.

Save the following code on your hard drive as jruby_basics.rb, in the same directory as junquenote_app.rb and jemmy.jar:[10]

`early_success/jruby_basics.rb`

```
require 'java'
require 'jemmy.jar'
require 'junquenote_app'

include_class 'org.netbeans.jemmy.JemmyProperties'
include_class 'org.netbeans.jemmy.TestOut'
```

❶
```
%w(Frame TextArea MenuBar Dialog Button).each do |o|
  include_class "org.netbeans.jemmy.operators.J#{o}Operator"
end
```

❷
❸
```
JemmyProperties.set_current_timeout 'DialogWaiter.WaitDialogTimeout', 3000
JemmyProperties.set_current_output TestOut.get_null_output

JunqueNoteApp.new
main_window = JFrameOperator.new 'JunqueNote'

puts "The main window's object ID is #{main_window.object_id}."
```

At ❶, we're pulling in all the Jemmy operators we'll need for this chapter. Rather than having a bunch of nearly identical include_class calls that differ by just a few characters, we've put the repetitive part of the code into a loop.

At ❷ and ❸, we set a couple of timing- and logging-related Jemmy configuration parameters. Notice how that JRuby allows you to call Java

---

10. http://www.netbeans.org/download/qa/jemmy.jar

methods like setCurrentTimeout() with more Ruby-like names such as set_current_timeout().

Go ahead and run what you have so far:

```
$ jruby jruby_basics.rb
```

You should now be looking at a JunqueNote window and a message on your command line. Success! Go ahead and shut down the app manually.

Keyboard Solo

It's time to give some life to the test script. Let's teach it to type text into the main window.

Unlike Win32, where you just type keystrokes and they land where they land, Jemmy directs keyboard input to whichever specific control you name. To get at the text area inside the window, we create a JTextArea-Operator.

The operator's typeText() method does all the work for us:

early_success/jruby_basics.rb

```
❶   edit = JTextAreaOperator.new main_window
❷   edit.type_text "this is some text"
```

You may have noticed in ❷ that we changed the method name to type_text(), with an underscore and different capitalization. As we discovered in the previous section, JRuby lets us use a more Ruby-friendly alternate spelling for any Java method. Since we're writing our test script in Ruby, we'll use the Ruby-style names from here on out.

The text area *belongs to* the main window, so at ❶, JTextAreaOperator takes its parent, main_window, as a parameter at creation time.

Run what you have so far. JunqueNote's main window should appear, and then its contents should change as if someone has been typing into it. You'll still need to close the window by hand, but we're about to fix that.

Quittin' Time!

If we can launch JunqueNote from a script, then we should be able to exit it from the same script. Lo and behold, the File menu has an Exit item. Let's use that.

Joe Asks...

Why Strings?

Why are we using strings to find menu items and dialog box controls? Doesn't that make our test script fragile in the face of international translations or the whims of the GUI designer?

We search for GUI objects by name because that's how the Jemmy API is written. No one says we have to hard-code our search strings, though. Using Jemmy's Bundle class, you could put your menu and button names in a property file...

```
junquenote.exit_menu=File|Exit
```

and use them like this:

```
include_class 'org.netbeans.jemmy.Bundle'

bundle = Bundle.new
bundle.load_from_file 'english.txt'
exit_menu = bundle.get_resource 'junquenote.exit_menu'

menu.push_menu_no_block exit_menu
```

I've skipped this step for the examples in this book to keep the source code brief (and because I'm pretty sure JunqueNote will never be translated to any other languages).

With Jemmy, we find menu items by their captions:

early_success/jruby_basics.rb

```
menu = JMenuBarOperator.new main_window
menu.push_menu_no_block 'File|Exit', '|'
```

Why is the method named push_menu_no_block()? That's a signal to Jemmy that we want our script to keep running without interruption.

As you've probably guessed, there's also a plain push_menu() method, but that one pauses the whole script until the app has completely finished responding to the menu. So it's suitable only for quick actions like Cut or Paste. Exiting the app is a potentially slow operation, because it brings up a "Do you want to save?" dialog box.

Speaking of the save prompt, we don't care about keeping our documents around just yet. So, we'll answer "No" for now, using another Jemmy operator to click the appropriate button.

We'll handle it like this:

`early_success/jruby_basics.rb`

```
dialog = JDialogOperator.new "Quittin' time"
button = JButtonOperator.new dialog, "No"
button.push
```

Now, when you run the script, the app should shut down for you.

2.4 Review

Whew! Just one chapter of code, and we've gotten a lot done already. We've launched the program we're testing, simulated typing, sent the command to exit the app, and sent mouse input to dismiss a dialog box. Twice!

Of course, we haven't written any tests yet, so we have no way of knowing whether the app is even doing its job. And our script is full of platform-specific API calls. It would be nice to be able to say something like the following without worrying about the specifics of the keystrokes or mouse events we're sending:

```
note.text = "This is a complete sentence."
```

or:

```
note.save_as 'MyNote'
```

We'll clear these hurdles in the upcoming chapters.

Listen to me. I'm should-ing all over myself.
▶ Al Franken

Chapter 3

Refactoring with RSpec

Now that we have a working script that drives an application, it might be tempting to jump right in and add some tests. After all, we know how to use platform calls like SendMessage() on Windows or typeText() on the Java runtime to make our test script push buttons and type keystrokes. We could just intersperse a few pass/fail checks in between all those function calls, right? Not so fast—let me tell you a story first. . . .

Write Once, Read Never

On one project, I inherited a bunch of old machine-written test scripts that had been generated by a capture/playback tool. Apparently, someone had long ago pressed Record in the capture tool and performed a bunch of tasks in the software they were testing. When they were done, the playback tool had generated a C program that, after a couple of tests were added, looked something like this:

```
MoveMouse(125, 163);
Delay(0.65);
LeftButtonDown();
Delay(0.074);
LeftButtonUp();
GetWindowText(hCtrl, buffer, bufferSize);
if (0 != lstrcmp(buffer, L"Some text"))
  LOG_FAILURE("Text didn't match\n");
Delay(0.687);
MoveMouse(204, 78);
//
// ...and so on, for pages and pages
```

What did this code even *do?* The capture/playback tool wasn't kind enough to write any comments (and how could it, anyway?).

The test script had been broken for a long time, because the GUI had gradually changed out from under it. Some buttons had moved slightly, and now the hard-coded mouse clicks in the test script fell on empty spaces. Other controls had migrated to completely different windows.

The new GUI was great for our customers, of course, since the software had become easier to use. But maintaining that spaghetti test code was a nightmare. The only way to figure out where to make changes was to run it until it broke, try tweaking the hard-coded pixel locations, and rerun it.

In the end, it was cheaper (and better for morale!) to scrap the test code than to continue trying to revive the dead script.

Even when they're carefully written by a real live human being, GUI tests can be hard to maintain, for two main reasons:

- *Lack of clarity*: You start with a short script, you keep adding a few tests at a time to the end, and soon you have a huge, amorphous blob of code. The tests at the end of the file might depend on something that happened at the very beginning, making it hard to reorganize the code later. And there's seldom any indication of *why* each click or keystroke is happening.
- *Fragility*: A lot of test scripts follow an alternating pattern: poke some buttons, check the results, poke more buttons, and so on. It's easy and tempting to mix details that might change with high-level concepts that will probably remain constant. But if the GUI designer changes the Search feature from a toolbar button to a menu item, you don't want to have to go through your entire script looking for places that need to be fixed.

How do we avoid those pitfalls? Instead of freely mixing pass/fail tests into our GUI automation code, we need to separate our concerns. The tests, which say *what* our application should do, belong in a different place from the Windows API calls, which say *how* it should do it.

In this chapter, we'll add the first batch of tests to our scripting project, but we're going to do it carefully and cleanly. All the tests will go into their own separate file to avoid the kind of coding chaos we saw in the earlier example.

Don't worry—we're not going to throw away all that working code we wrote in the ..._basics.rb files from the previous chapter. Quite the contrary! We're going to lavish it with attention and put it into a Ruby class to make it easier to call from our tests.

First, though, we'll direct our focus to the tests themselves. We want the intent behind the test code to be crystal clear to whoever is reading or maintaining it—which will probably be us. So, let's treat ourselves to some beautiful source code. We're going to write our tests using a dedicated test description language (built on Ruby!) called RSpec.

3.1 RSpec: The Language of Lucid Tests

Let's talk for a minute about the art of writing good test scripts. If we want our test code to be clear, it should be written in the application's problem domain—that is, using the same concepts that end users see when they use the software. In the case of LockNote, we should write scripts that deal in documents and passwords, not menu IDs and edit controls.

We also want to keep our test script from becoming one long, tangled, interdependent mess. So, we'll start with small, self-contained tests. Once we have confidence in our building blocks, we can assemble them into more meaningful tests.

During this process, it's helpful to think of these little units of test code as *examples* of correct behavior. I really mean it when I say we're going to start small. Our first examples will fit on a cocktail napkin.

The Napkin

Imagine that you're sitting down for coffee with your software designers, chatting about how the program is going to work. Someone grabs a napkin, everyone huddles around talking and sketching excitedly, and you end up with something like Figure 3.1, on the following page.

That kind of simplicity is just for sketches, right? Surely we have to abandon such hand-wavy descriptions when we actually start implementing our tests.

But what if we *could* write our test code the same way we wrote those notes on the napkin?

```
describe the main window
  it launches with a welcome message
  it exits without a prompt if nothing has changed
  it prompts before exiting if the document has changed
```

With just a handful of little examples like these, we could write about facets of our application's behavior in a specialized test description language. The language is easy to write and clear to read. There's just one problem: how do we get from paper to practice?

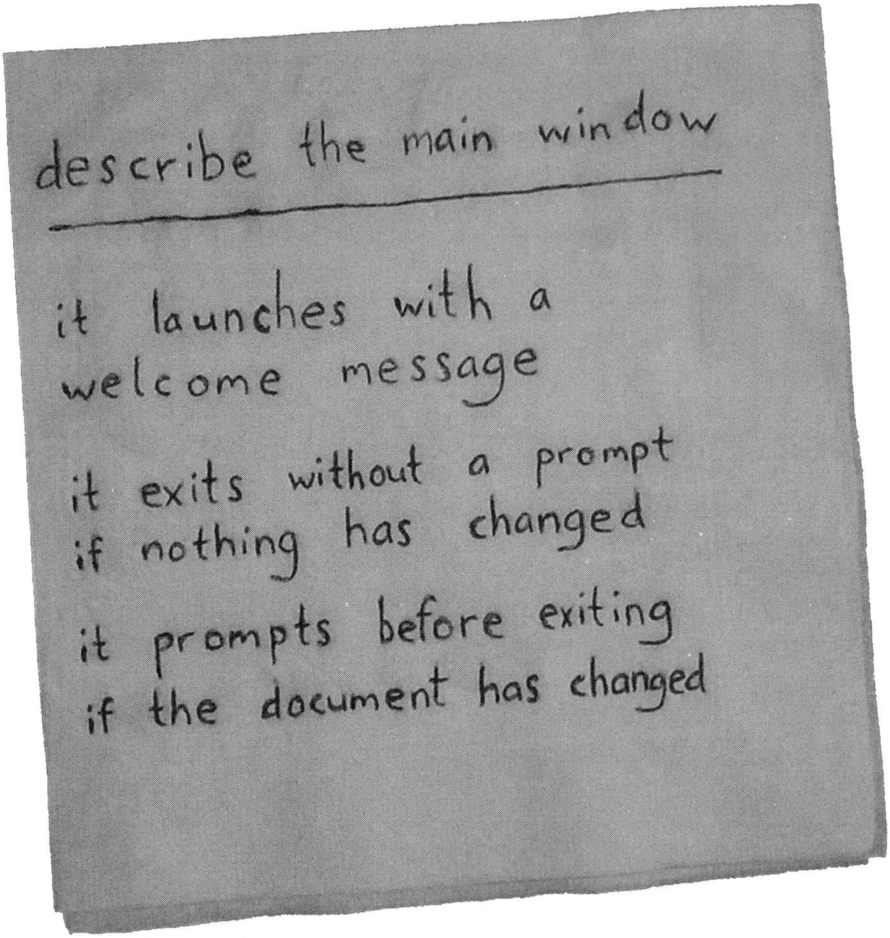

Figure 3.1: THE ULTIMATE REQUIREMENTS CAPTURE TOOL

> \\//
> ؟ʃ **Joe Asks...**
>
> ### What Will This Buy Me?
>
> What kinds of bugs will tests catch at this level of detail? Bad requirements, for one. When you fill in the bodies of those examples, your team will be forced to consider all kinds of usability edge cases as you describe how the app is really going to work.
>
> You don't *need* a test script to do that. A sharp eye and empathy for your customer will help unearth the same kinds of issues.
>
> But if you do choose to express your ideas as running code, you can press it into service later in the project as an automated "smoke test" that runs every time a developer checks in code.

Introducing RSpec

The notation we've been using on this napkin is as real as Ruby. It's called RSpec.[1] It's implemented as a Ruby library, but you can also think of it as a language of its own—a *test description language* that just happens to be built on Ruby's strong metaprogramming foundation.[2]

The philosophy behind RSpec is that a good test should do more than exercise the code; it should also communicate its intentions clearly. RSpec provides two motifs for helping us write clear tests:

- The describe/it notation provides an overall structure for your test script.

- The should verb is how you write the individual pass/fail tests.

describe/it

A few paragraphs ago, we saw that a good test script is more like a series of *examples* of correct behavior than an exhaustive specification. RSpec encourages this view of testing. Each example in RSpec is expressed as a sentence beginning with it, as in "it self-destructs when I hit the red button." We gather each group of related examples that describe one feature in, fittingly enough, a describe block.

---

1. http://rspec.rubyforge.org
2. *Metaprogramming* is simply "programs writing programs." It's the technique that makes Ruby such a great platform for coders to build their own languages.

```
describe 'The main window' do
  it 'launches with a welcome message'
  it 'exits without a prompt if nothing has changed'
  it 'prompts before exiting if the document has changed'
end
```

Figure 3.2: THE NAPKIN, TRANSLATED INTO RSPEC

It takes only a few keystrokes to transform our cocktail napkin into a set of RSpec examples, as in Figure 3.2.

The code looks almost like it depends on some kind of fancy English language processing, but really it's just Ruby. describe() and it() are plain ol' Ruby functions supplied by the RSpec library.

We'll eventually fill in each of those it descriptions with specific tests, with help from RSpec's should idiom.

should

In some testing toolkits, you're expected to use a system of "assertions" to write your pass/fail tests, something like this:

```
ASSERT_EQUAL(windowTitle, "My Program");
```

RSpec is a little different. Rather than asking you to make your style of writing more like programming, it bends the programming language to look more like natural writing. The previous example would look like this in RSpec:

```
window_title.should == 'My Program'
```

"Window title should equal 'My Program.'" You could practically read this code aloud. You could even show it to someone who's never seen Ruby before, and they'd probably understand what it does.

With RSpec, the should() and should_not() methods are available to every object in Ruby.[3] All of the following are valid tests in RSpec:

```
(2 + 2).should == 4
1.should be < 2
['this', 'list'].should_not be_empty
{:color => 'red'}.should have_key(:color)
```

---

3. Thanks to Ruby's "open classes," whose definitions can be modified on the fly. This flexibility is what makes RSpec possible.

Any test written with should() will raise an exception (and show up in the test report as a failed test) if its condition turns out to be false. Similarly, its companion method, should_not(), fails on true conditions.

Take a look at those last two tests. be_empty tells RSpec to call the empty?() method of the array. have_key calls the hash table's has_key?() method. This technique works for *any* method, not just empty?(). In general, be_*xyz* calls xyz?(), and have_*xyz* calls has_xyz?().

Trying It

Let's grab the RSpec library and take it for a test-drive:

```
C:\> gem install rspec
```

Now our cocktail napkin translation is more than just a nicely formatted description of behavior. It's running code—try it! Save the code snippet (from Figure 3.2, on the facing page) as note_spec.rb, and run it with the spec executable, like this:

```
C:\> spec --format specdoc note_spec.rb
```

```
The main window
- launches with a welcome message (PENDING: Not Yet Implemented)
- exits without a prompt if nothing has changed (PENDING: Not Yet Implemented)
- prompts before exiting if the document has changed (PENDING: Not Yet Implemented)

Finished in 0.017212 seconds

3 examples, 0 failures, 3 pending
...
```

RSpec has noticed that our tests haven't been implemented yet. But we've definitely made progress. Three empty tests are better than no tests at all. Now, let's fill in those details.

Putting It to Work

So far, our test script is merely an outline of what we will be doing. It describes which parts of the program we're testing, but it doesn't contain any pass/fail tests yet. Let's change that.

Remember our cautionary tale from the beginning of the chapter? We want to write our tests in the vocabulary of LockNote or JunqueNote and leave the platform-specific calls for a different part of the code. So, we're going to imagine that someone has lovingly provided a note-taking API just for us and code to that API. (Guess who's going to "lovingly provide" this API? Heaven helps those who help themselves. . . .)

Replace the first it clause in your script with the following:

```
with_rspec/note_spec.rb
```

```
it 'launches with a welcome message' do
❶    note = Note.new
❷    note.text.should include('Welcome')
❸    note.exit!
end
```

The code at ❶ will create a new window (by launching the application). We'll add the implementation in a few minutes, using the automation techniques from the previous chapter.

At ❷, we add our first actual pass/fail test. We want to make sure the word "Welcome" appears somewhere in the editable portion of the main window.

Finally, we shut down the app at ❸. We'll follow the Ruby tradition of giving "dangerous" methods like exit!() an exclamation point. We want whoever is reading this code to know that the exiting program will discard the active document and steamroller over any save prompts along the way.

Now, when we run our script, we see the following:

```
1)
NameError in 'The main window launches with a welcome message'
uninitialized constant Note

...
```

No surprise there. We've started tossing around this new term in our code, Note, without telling Ruby what it is. It's time to teach Ruby all about our note taking.

3.2 Building a Library

Up to this point, we've been working downward from our high-level test concepts to the specifics of LockNote and JunqueNote. Now it's time to build upward from the Windows and Java API calls we learned in Chapter 2, *An Early Success*, on page 11. We're going to put that low-level code together into a coherent library usable from our tests.

We want to do for our GUI tests what RSpec's creators did for testing in general: provide a way to express concepts clearly. RSpec will be our "gold standard" of beauty: we're going to shoot for a note-taking API clean enough to be at home inside an RSpec test.

A Touch of Class

The code we need to implement a clean API is already there in our two
..._basics.rb files; it just needs to be touched up a bit and organized into
a Ruby class. We'll start with an empty class called Note in a new file
named after the app we're testing (locknote.rb or junquenote.rb):

```
class Note
end
```

Later, we'll add each chunk of platform-specific calls as we find a good
home for it.

To tell RSpec which program we're testing, we pass the name of the app
with the -r option. So on Windows, we have this:

```
C:\> spec -rlocknote -fs note_spec.rb
```

And for the cross-platform version, we have this:

```
$ jruby -S spec -rjunquenote -fs note_spec.rb
```

What are the results when we try it?

```
1)
NoMethodError in 'The main window launches with a welcome message'
undefined method `text' for #<Note:0x1016e1c>
```

As we expected, RSpec was able to create a Note object, but it couldn't
do anything more. We haven't yet taught it to get the current document's text. In fact, we haven't even taught it to launch the application
yet. Let's do so now.

Starting Up

Reorganizing the code into a class will be pretty much the same whether
you're playing the Windows or JRuby version of our home game.

Creating a new Note object should cause the app to launch. So, we'll
move our window creation code from the previous chapter into Note's
initialize() method:

```
«platform definitions»

class Note
  def initialize
    «code up through the first `puts`»
  end

  «more to come...»
end
```

I won't show all the code here, because it's nearly an exact repeat of what you wrote in the previous chapter. You just put all your require lines (and Jemmy imports, for you JRuby readers) into the "platform definitions" section at the top and paste everything else up to the first puts into the body of initialize( ).

We'll use the main_window variable in some of the other methods we're defining, so we need to "promote" it to an attribute of the Note class. Replace main_window with @main_window everywhere you see it.

Now that we've taught our Note class how to launch the app, let's move on to text entry.

Typing Into the Window

You've already written the code to simulate typing. It just needs to be made a bit more general. Grab the handful of lines that deal with keyboard input—look for "this is some text"—and paste them into a new type_in( ) method inside the Note class:

```
def type_in(message)
  «typing code here»
end
```

Of course, you'll probably want to replace the *"this is some text"* string literal with the message parameter that our top-level test script passes in. That takes care of writing text—how about reading it back?

Getting Text Back from the Window

Up until now, we've been driving the GUI from our script, but we haven't retrieved any data from it yet. To change that state of affairs, we'll need one more platform-specific technique. It's an easy one, though, so I'm going to present the Windows and JRuby variants back-to-back.

Windows: The WM_GETTEXT Message

First, we want to drill down into LockNote's user interface and find the editable area that contains the document's text. This text area is a *child window* of the main window. To grab hold of it, we'll use FindWindowEx( ). It's like the FindWindow( ) function we used before, but with a couple of extra parameters—including the parent window option we need.

Once we've found the edit control, we'll send it the WM_GETTEXT message to find out what's inside it. You've seen the PostMessage( ) call for sending a message to a window. Its cousin SendMessage( ) is similar but is guaranteed to wait until the window actually *responds* to our message.

Joe Asks...

What's the Significance of the Window Class?

In the previous chapter, we mentioned that a *window class* identifies whether a given window is a button, edit control, dialog box, or whatnot.

The basic controls that come with Windows have names like edit or button. This window class's name, ATL:00434310, is a little more complicated—it's a customization from Microsoft's open source Windows Template Library, used by LockNote's developers to write the application.

The meanings of SendMessage()'s parameters are different for every Windows message. For WM_GETTEXT, the last two parameters are the maximum size string we can accept and a pointer to the string where we want Windows to put the text we're asking for.

Here's what these two new API calls look like in use. Add the following code inside your LockNote class:

`with_rspec/locknote.rb`

```ruby
def text
  find_window_ex = user32 'FindWindowEx', ['L', 'L', 'P', 'P'], 'L'

  send_message = user32 'SendMessage', ['L', 'L', 'L', 'P'], 'L'

  edit = find_window_ex.call @main_window, 0, 'ATL:00434310', nil

❶ buffer = '\0' * 2048
  send_message.call edit, WM_GETTEXT, buffer.length, buffer

  return buffer
end
```

As another concession to the manual memory management of the Windows world, we have to presize our buffer at ❶, just like we did with get_window_rect() in the previous chapter.

JRuby: The text Property

The JRuby approach to getting text is similar to the Windows one: we look for the editable text area (which belongs to the main window) and quiz it about its contents. Jemmy's JTextAreaOperator provides the text property for this purpose:

`with_rspec/junquenote.rb`

```
def text
❶   edit = JTextAreaOperator.new @main_window
    edit.text
end
```

The code at ❶ should look familiar; the type_in() method you wrote in the previous section contains one just like it. This is a sign that our code needs some cleanup, which we'll get to in the next chapter.

Closing the Window

OK, Windows and Swing readers should both be ready for one final step in this chapter. Paste the remainder of your code into this skeleton:

```
def exit!
❶   begin
      «remainder of code»

❷     @prompted = true
❸   rescue
    end
end
```

Windows users, you'll have to add one extra line at ❶: paste in the definition of find_window() again just before the begin. We'll remove the need for this repetition soon.

Our higher-level test code will need to know if the program prompted us to save our document. So, we're going to wait for a few seconds for a save prompt to appear. If we see a prompt, we remember this event in the @prompted attribute at ❷. If not, we'll get a TimeoutError (or NativeException in JRuby).

An exception isn't necessarily a bad thing in this case. It could be that we're exiting the app without changing anything—no need for a save prompt then. We just catch the exception at ❸, and @prompted stays nil.

So, how do we use @prompted in our test script? As we discussed earlier, any test that reads should have_xyz will call a function named has_xyz?() and check its return value for true or false/nil.

```
def has_prompted?
  @prompted
end
```

Two More Tests

We now have all the tools required to fill in the other two examples:

`with_rspec/note_spec.rb`

```ruby
it 'exits without a prompt if nothing has changed' do
  note = Note.new
  note.exit!
  note.should_not have_prompted
end

it 'prompts before exiting if the document has changed' do
  note = Note.new
  note.type_in "changed"
  note.exit!
  note.should have_prompted
end
```

There you have it: one cocktail napkin turned into a working test plan.

3.3 The Story So Far

At last, we have a test script that actually runs some tests! And they're written in a clear language free of platform-specific API jargon. Simple Ruby code exercises the user interface, and RSpec's should verb tells us whether it responded correctly.

We've also managed to avoid the maintenance trap of bogging down our top-level test code with details like window or menu captions. Of course, those specific API calls like FindWindow() and pushMenu() had to go *somewhere*. We kept them out of our main test script, note_spec.rb, but they're still lurking in the supporting Note class inside locknote.rb and junquenote.rb.

So, now the Note class has two kinds of code in it: general GUI function definitions (which are reusable from project to project) and the "note-taking API" (which we created just for this project). In the next chapter, we'll move the reusable parts into their own file. Not only will this change help us in future projects, but it will be handy for *this* one. We're about to teach our Note class a few new tricks, and we don't want them to get lost in the noise.

Programs must be written for people to read, and only incidentally for machines to execute.

▶ Abelson and Sussman, **Structure and Interpretation of Computer Programs**

Chapter 4

Next Iteration: Simplify!

Have you ever put up wallpaper in a house? Sometimes, an air bubble gets trapped under the paper. You mash your thumb down on it with satisfaction, but you haven't really eliminated it. You've just moved it elsewhere.

Software complexity is kind of like that, too. We spent the entire previous chapter building a clean test script that was free of the mundane details of platform API definitions. But they're still hiding out in our project, cluttering up our Note class.

If you think about it, the bindings to the Windows environment are pretty much the same, no matter which project they're being used in. And you could say the same for the Java runtime ones. So, why don't we move these platform bindings to their own file that we can use in future projects?

What we want to do is separate the code that deals with text editing in general from the code that deals in platform API calls. We'll split the Note class into layers, something like Figure 4.1, on the following page. In this chapter, we're going to fill in all three of those layers.[1]

We'll start by putting the barest Note skeleton into note.rb. Then we'll take on the left and right halves of the diagram in separate Windows and JRuby tracks. As we learn new low-level GUI calls and then apply them in our project, we'll be bouncing back and forth between (for example) windows_gui.rb and locknote.rb. To help keep things straight, I've marked each code sample with the file it came from.

---

1. Why three layers instead of just two? The topmost layer holds code common to the Windows and Swing apps. If your project is a single-platform one, you won't need it.

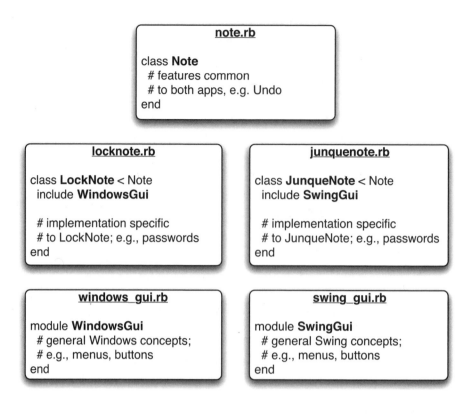

Figure 4.1: THE THREE LAYERS

By the end of the chapter, we'll have enough tools to unify the two worlds somewhat.

4.1 Abstracting the Common Code

Here's the skeleton of Note with the platform-specific code removed:

`simplify/note.rb`

```
class Note
❶    @@app = nil
❷    @@titles = {}

    def self.open
      @@app.new
    end
end
```

We don't want our top-level test script to have to say LockNote.new or JunqueNote.new. Instead, we'll provide a generic open() method that will automatically create a new LockNote or JunqueNote object, depending on which platform we're running on.[2]

There are about a zillion ways to do this. The simplest for now is just to keep around an attribute called @@app at ❶ to store the name of the class that controls the application. (While we're in this part of the code, we'll also add a @@titles collection for dialog box titles, which will come in handy later.)

Everywhere our RSpec script used to say Note.new, it's going to say Note.open instead. locknote.rb and junquenote.rb will each contain a line specifying which Note implementation open() should use, followed by a list of dialog box titles that are specific to the app.

The code is nearly identical for both programs, so I'll just show the version inside LockNote:

`simplify/locknote.rb`
```
@@app = LockNote
@@titles[:save] = 'Steganos LockNote'
```

It doesn't seem like much of a start, but we have enough of a foundation to build up our entire application's behavior.

So, now we'll turn our attention to the platform-specific parts of the implementation. One more time, we're going to deal with this part of the reorganization effort in separate Windows and JRuby sections.

4.2 Cleaning Windows

Let's start with those Win32 API calls. Their definitions are scattered all over the place and sometimes even repeated. Using them is kind of a chore. They're not really functions, so we can invoke them only using their call() method. If only they were real Ruby methods so that we could gather them into a module and include them into LockNote....

Special Promotion

We'd like to figure out a way to "promote" a Win32API object to a method. The naïve way to do it would be to wrap each object in a method.

---

2. Fans of design patterns are jumping on their chairs yelling, "Factory! Factory! Factory!" right about now.

```ruby
def find_window(wnd_class, title)
  @find_window_api ||= Win32API.new \
    'user32', 'FindWindow', ['P', 'P'], 'L'

  @find_window_api.call wnd_class, title
end
```

This is a decent first start, but we're repeating the name of the Windows function in no fewer than four places! And we'd have to repeat this *structure*, too, for each API function we want to use. How do we DRY up this code?[3] By specifying only the parts unique to each function— something like this:

`simplify/windows_gui.rb`

```ruby
module WindowsGui
  def_api 'FindWindow',    ['P', 'P'], 'L'
  def_api 'keybd_event',   ['I', 'I', 'L', 'L'], 'V'

  # rest of API definitions here...

  WM_GETTEXT = 0x000D
  WM_SYSCOMMAND = 0x0112

  # rest of constant definitions here...
end
```

def_api() would do the heavy lifting of creating the Win32API object and somehow adding a new Ruby method that calls it. But def_api() doesn't exist. We're going to have to write it.

RSpec to the Rescue, Again

How exactly should def_api() work? Let's express our intent as a series of real, runnable RSpec examples:

`simplify/windows_gui_spec.rb`

```ruby
require 'windows_gui'

❶ describe WindowsGui do
  include WindowsGui

  it 'wraps a Windows call with a method' do
❷    find_window(nil, nil).should_not == 0
  end

  it 'enforces the argument count' do
❸    lambda {find_window}.should raise_error
  end
end
```

---

3. DRY = "Don't Repeat Yourself." See http://c2.com/cgi/wiki?DontRepeatYourself.

FindWindow() will do for a guinea pig. We've already defined it in our excerpt from windows_gui.rb earlier, so our test can just go ahead and call it.

First, we'll try an example of normal find_window() usage at ❷. Passing it two nils is guaranteed to return *some* top-level window's handle.

But we also want to make sure def_api() does some rudimentary parameter checking, so our tests will also try calling find_window() incorrectly. You can pronounce the lambda at ❸ as, "The code that…". So, the whole line reads, "The code that calls find_window() with no arguments should raise an error."

At ❶, we see that describe can take a Ruby class name as its parameter, as an alternative to the free-form string names we used for descriptions in the previous chapter. It doesn't make too much difference either way; using a class name is perhaps a little cleaner.

Home and DRY

Of course, we still have to write def_api():

`simplify/windows_gui.rb`

```
require 'Win32API'

module WindowsGui
❶   def self.def_api(function, parameters, return_value)
      api = Win32API.new 'user32', function, parameters, return_value

❷     define_method(function.snake_case) do |*args|
❸       api.call *args
      end
    end
end
```

Don't miss the self keyword at ❶, since def_api() is a class-level method.

❷ is where the real magic happens. define_method() is Ruby's secret sauce for adding methods to classes on the fly, at runtime, without even knowing the function name ahead of time.

That's a good thing, too, because we're *calculating* those names. We're transforming Windows-style, mixed-case identifiers (known as *CamelCase*) into the more Ruby-like, underscored (aka *snake_case*) ones. We'll write that translation code in a minute.

We first encountered the "flexible number of parameters" asterisk in Section 2.2, *Clicking the Button*, on page 22. We're using it again at ❷.

We get all the passed-in arguments packed into one array, and at ❸, we expand them into multiple arguments for the Windows API call.

Now, about those function names. . . .

Yak Shaving

Since function renaming is at heart just a string translation, let's add a snake_case() method to the String class. We want it to convert CamelCase text but leave alone text that's already in snake_case.

We'll document our expectations in RSpec; this is becoming an epic bout of yak shaving![4]

`simplify/windows_gui_spec.rb`

```
describe String, '#snake_case' do
  it 'transforms CamelCase strings' do
    'GetCharWidth32'.snake_case.should == 'get_char_width_32'
  end

  it 'leaves snake_case strings intact' do
    'keybd_event'.snake_case.should == 'keybd_event'
  end
end
```

snake_case() is actually pretty easy to write. We'll use a regular expression to look for a lowercase letter followed by a number or uppercase letter (a few rare Windows calls end in numbers). Just above your implementation of def_api(), put the following code:

`simplify/windows_gui.rb`

```
class String
  def snake_case
❶   gsub(/([a-z])([A-Z0-9])/, '\1_\2').downcase
  end
end
```

Did it work? Let's find out:

```
C:\> spec -fs windows_gui_spec.rb

WindowsGui
- wraps a Windows call with a method
- enforces the argument count
```

---

4. *Yak shaving* is working on a task that, although important, is several steps removed from our goal, such as putting off our GUI script work—to write a test—for a conversion of a function name—from an API—in a utility class.

```
String#snake_case
- modifies CamelCase strings
- leaves snake_case strings intact

Finished in 0.581 seconds

4 examples, 0 failures
```

Huzzah!

The Keyboard Revisited

Let's turn our attention to the keyboard. In Section 2.2, *Typing Text*, on page 18, we threw in a quick hack to type lowercase letters. But what about numbers, capital letters, spaces, and so on? It's time to give type_in() a little love.

Press and Release

How do we type a capital *A*? We hold down the Shift key, press and release the A key, and finally release the Shift key.[5]

Capital letters aren't the only things that require multiple keys to be pressed at once. Keyboard shortcuts like Ctrl+A and many punctuation characters also need them. So, let us then imagine a "compound keystroke" function we'd use like this...

```
keystroke VK_CONTROL, 'a'
```

assuming we've defined the Windows codes for the modifier keys as building blocks:

simplify/windows_gui.rb
```
module WindowsGui
  VK_SHIFT   = 0x10
  VK_CONTROL = 0x11
  VK_BACK    = 0x08
end
```

How will we implement this function? Just like human fingers would, our code will press and hold each key in order and then release them in reverse order.

---

5. Or we turn on Caps Lock, but that's outside the scope of this book. From here on out, we're assuming Caps Lock is off.

```
simplify/windows_gui.rb
```
```ruby
module WindowsGui
  def keystroke(*keys)
    return if keys.empty?

    keybd_event keys.first, 0, KEYEVENTF_KEYDOWN, 0
    sleep 0.05
    keystroke *keys[1..-1]
    sleep 0.05
    keybd_event keys.first, 0, KEYEVENTF_KEYUP, 0
  end
end
```

That takes care of typing a single character, once we know what keys
we have to press in order to type it.

From Character to Keystrokes

How do we get from the concept of a *character* to a series of key codes?
By extending String to do this translation for us:

```
simplify/windows_gui.rb
```
```ruby
class String
  def to_keys
❶    unless size == 1
      raise "conversion is for single characters only"
    end

❷    ascii = unpack('C')[0]

❸    case self
    when '0'..'9'
      [ascii - ?0 + 0x30]
    when 'A'..'Z'
      [WindowsGui.const_get(:VK_SHIFT), ascii]
    when 'a'..'z'
      [ascii - ?a + ?A]
    when ' '
      [ascii]
    else
      raise "Can't convert unknown character #{self}"
    end
  end
end
```

Recall that in Ruby, single characters and strings are the same data
type, so we'll do a quick length check at ❶ to make sure we're dealing
with one character at a time.

At ❷, we base our calculation on the ASCII code for the character. This simplistic method will be fine as long as we narrow our examples to 1-byte characters like the ones my U.S. English keyboard can type. For international text, see the emerging Ruby 1.9 work, or use one of the Unicode add-ons for Ruby 1.8.

❸ is where we translate the various characters into their virtual key codes, based on the API documentation.[6] These particular keystrokes are fairly standard, but if you ever add more punctuation characters to this function, take caution. Different international keyboard layouts may use different keystrokes to represent a given character.

From here, implementing type_in() is a simple matter. First, we move it into WindowsGui alongside its Windows API friends. Inside the method, we use String#scan() to call keystroke() once for each character:

`simplify/windows_gui.rb`

```ruby
module WindowsGui
  def type_in(message)
    message.scan(/./m) do |char|
      keystroke(*char.to_keys)
    end
  end
end
```

Our keyboard entry code is now both more complete and cleaner than it was a few minutes ago. There's just one last section of LockNote that needs tidying.

Pain-Free Windows

The methods that open and close LockNote were pretty long in the previous chapter. Most of the code was low-level stuff about dialog boxes and mouse coordinates. Let's get that code into WindowsGui where it belongs.

Slim Packaging

We'll start simply with a new Window class, which will just be a thin wrapper around a window handle.

---

6. http://msdn.microsoft.com/en-us/library/ms645540.aspx

Put the following definition inside WindowsGui:

```
simplify/windows_gui.rb
module WindowsGui
  class Window
❶   include WindowsGui

    attr_reader :handle

    def initialize(handle)
      @handle = handle
    end

    def close
      post_message @handle, WM_SYSCOMMAND, SC_CLOSE, 0
    end

❷   def wait_for_close
      timeout(5) do
        sleep 0.2 until 0 == is_window_visible(@handle)
      end
    end

    def text
      buffer = '\0' * 2048
      length = send_message @handle, WM_GETTEXT, buffer.length, buffer
      length == 0 ? '' : buffer[0..length - 1]
    end
  end
end
```

You may have noticed at ❶ that we're including WindowsGui inside a class that's nested in WindowsGui. This might well seem a little circular, but I promise it will work. All those API calls we need will get imported just fine.

The other thing we've added is a wait_for_close() method at ❷, which in turn relies on another Windows API call, IsWindowVisible(). This function takes a window handle and returns an integer. Take a shot at defining it with def_api()—how does your version compare to the one in this chapter's source code?

Keeping Up Appearances

Creating a new Window requires a window handle. But where do we get the window handle in the first place?

There are two ways. For a top-level window like LockNote's main window, we typically wait in a loop until the window appears. So, let's add a class-level method to do that. The code is the same loop construct we wrote two chapters ago:

```
simplify/windows_gui.rb
class WindowsGui::Window
❶    extend WindowsGui

    def self.top_level(title, seconds=3)
      @handle = timeout(seconds) do
        sleep 0.2 while (h = find_window nil, title) <= 0; h
      end

      Window.new @handle
    end
end
```

Why are we referencing WindowsGui at ❶? Didn't we already do that? Yes, but just for instance methods. This time, we're making Windows-Gui's methods available to *class-level* methods of Window.

The other way to get a window handle is to look inside a parent window for child controls. Just for fun, we'll allow searching by title, window class, or control ID:

```
simplify/windows_gui.rb
class WindowsGui::Window
  def child(id)
    result = case id
    when String
❶      by_title = find_window_ex @handle, 0, nil, id.gsub('_', '&')
      by_class = find_window_ex @handle, 0, id, nil
      by_title > 0 ? by_title : by_class
    when Fixnum
      get_dlg_item @handle, id
    else
      0
    end

    raise "Control '#{id}' not found" if result == 0
    Window.new result
  end
end
```

One thing to note on searching by title: control names like "Yes" are actually stored by Windows as *&Yes*, with the first character of their keyboard shortcut marked with an ampersand. (This difference is one of many reasons it's better to use control IDs.) In a nod to clarity, we'll allow callers to use underscores instead of ampersands; it's easy enough to add a translation at ❶.

Now that we have the general concept of windows, we'll move on to dialog boxes.

A Meaningful Dialog (Box)

A dialog box is just a top-level window that is on the screen only for a short term. Ruby has a convention for this kind of short-lived object. Just like File#open() keeps a file open for the duration of one block only, we want to be able to write dialog box code like this:

```
dialog('Are you sure?') do |dialog|
  # do stuff with dialog,
  # including clicking OK
end

# Ruby waits until the dialog is closed
# before continuing here
```

It's easy to write an implementation that fits this pattern. All we need to do is yield a Window object to the code that called us:

```
simplify/windows_gui.rb
module WindowsGui
  def dialog(title, seconds=3)
    d = begin
      w = Window.top_level(title, seconds)
❶     yield(w) ? w : nil
    rescue TimeoutError
    end

    d.wait_for_close if d
    return d
  end
end
```

And just like exit!() in the previous chapter, dialog() won't throw an exception if the window never appears. It will just return a Window object (which will evaluate to true) or nil.

The code at ❶ lets us bail out of closing, if we *really* want to force it to stay open. There's one edge case in the next chapter where we'll need to do exactly that.

Clicking the Window Shut

The rectangle and mouse-clicking code is nearly the same as before. All we need to do is make the hard-coded IDNO control ID into a parameter.

`simplify/windows_gui.rb`

```ruby
class WindowsGui::Window
  def click(id)
    h = child(id).handle

    rectangle = [0, 0, 0, 0].pack 'LLLL'
    get_window_rect h, rectangle
    left, top, right, bottom = rectangle.unpack 'LLLL'

    center = [(left + right) / 2, (top + bottom) / 2]
    set_cursor_pos *center

    mouse_event MOUSEEVENTF_LEFTDOWN, 0, 0, 0, 0
    mouse_event MOUSEEVENTF_LEFTUP, 0, 0, 0, 0
  end
end
```

With all these improvements, LockNote's initialize() function is now a three-liner:

`simplify/locknote.rb`

```ruby
require 'windows_gui'
require 'note'

class LockNote < Note
  include WindowsGui

  @@app = LockNote
  @@titles[:save] = 'Steganos LockNote'

  def initialize
    system 'start "" "C:/LockNote/LockNote.exe"'

    @main_window = Window.top_level 'LockNote - Steganos LockNote'
    @edit_window = @main_window.child 'ATL:00434310'
  end
end
```

And entering text is just a matter of keystrokes:

`simplify/locknote.rb`

```ruby
class LockNote
  def text
    @edit_window.text
  end

  def text=(message)
    keystroke VK_CONTROL, ?A
    keystroke VK_BACK
    type_in(message)
  end
end
```

Exiting the app doesn't contain any platform code at all anymore, so it's moved out of LockNote entirely. See Section 4.4, *Satisfaction*, on page 58 for the definition.

4.3 Polishing JRuby

We don't have much work to do to hide the details of Swing GUIs from the rest of our code. Jemmy already presents a pretty clean interface for opening windows and typing characters.

So, we won't be building up an abstraction, the way we did for Windows; we'll be *adapting* one.

Getting Started

Note's open() method creates a new JunqueNote object. We need to fill in its initializer:

`simplify/junquenote.rb`

```
❶  require 'swing_gui'
   require 'junquenote_app'
   require 'note'

   class JunqueNote < Note
     include SwingGui

     @@app = JunqueNote
     @@titles[:save] = "Quittin' time"

     def initialize
       JunqueNoteApp.new

       @main_window = JFrameOperator.new 'JunqueNote'
❷      @edit_window = JTextAreaOperator.new @main_window
     end
   end
```

This is almost identical to how we created a new JunqueNote object in the previous chapter. Only two things are different.

At ❶, we're including a new swing_gui.rb file, which will contain all those import and include_class directives that plug us into the Java runtime.

In Section 3.2, *JRuby: The text Property*, on page 39, the line that finds the edit control was duplicated in every method that needed it. If we put the line at ❷ instead, it needs to appear in our script only once.

Getting Text

Now that @edit_window is part of the JunqueNote class, getting text into and out of the window is much simpler:

```
simplify/junquenote.rb
class JunqueNote
  def text
    @edit_window.text
  end

  def text=(message)
    @edit_window.clear_text
    @edit_window.type_text message
  end
end
```

And that just leaves the topic of, well, leaving.

Getting Out

Our top-level test script is going to attempt to close the program's main window, wait for a confirmation dialog box, and click a No button—all without knowing on which platform it's running.

So, our Swing GUI adapter is going to have to fulfill three expectations:

1. The main window needs a close() method to signal that we're exiting the program. We're already covered here, since JFrameOperator comes out of the box with this feature.

2. The JunqueNote object needs a dialog() method that waits for a dialog box to show, runs some caller-supplied code, and returns true if the dialog box indeed appeared. We'll have to add this method ourselves.

3. The dialog() method exposes some kind of object that supports a click() operation.

First, let's look at dialog().

It belongs to JunqueNote for this project, but we'd like to be able to use it in *any* project. So, we'll put it in a SwingGui module that can be mixed into any class.

simplify/swing_gui.rb

```ruby
module SwingGui
  def dialog(title, seconds=3)
    JemmyProperties.set_current_timeout \
      'DialogWaiter.WaitDialogTimeout', seconds * 1000

    begin
      d = JDialogOperator.new title
❶     yield d
      d.wait_closed

      true
    rescue NativeException
    end
  end
end
```

At ❶, we pass the JDialogOperator object back to the caller to run whatever code he wants. The only thing we need to guarantee is that the object supports a click() method:

simplify/swing_gui.rb

```ruby
class JDialogOperator
  def click(title)
❶   b = JButtonOperator.new self, title.gsub('_', '')
    b.push
  end
end
```

Why are we removing underscores from the button name at ❶? In the notation of our generic Note class, we use an underscore to indicate which character in the name carries the keyboard shortcut (for example, _No means "N is for No"). But Jemmy doesn't care about shortcuts for buttons, so we strip out this extra information.

With these two additions, we've successfully adapted our Swing interface to a generic one.

4.4 Satisfaction

We've spent a while developing Windows and Swing abstractions separately. It's time to take a first step at reuniting the two camps. The code for this section is going to go into the Note class inside note.rb, because LockNote and JunqueNote are both going to use it.

Ready for our first piece of common GUI code?

`simplify/note.rb`

```ruby
class Note
  def exit!
    @main_window.close

❶   @prompted = dialog(@@titles[:save]) do |d|
      d.click '_No'
    end
  end

  def has_prompted?
    @prompted
  end
end
```

Each app has its own title for the "Do you want to save first?" dialog box, so we use the @@titles attribute at ❶ to keep the code nice and generic.

It may not feel like we've accomplished much in this chapter. After all, our test script doesn't behave differently than it did before all this reorganization. But look at locknote.rb, for instance. It's gone from 130-odd lines of Windows definitions mixed with LockNote concepts to fewer than 40 lines of targeted, application-specific code. Sure, windows_gui.rb is a bit hefty, but we're going to be able to reuse that part of the code in other projects.

More important, the building blocks of keystrokes and dialog boxes are now in good enough shape that we can plunge right into implementing the next round of tests.

A poem is never finished, only abandoned.
 ▶ Paul Valéry

Chapter 5

The Home Stretch

We now have everything we need to write good examples for the rest of the features of LockNote and JunqueNote. Over the past few chapters, we've built a solid connection to the underlying platform API, found a clean abstraction of the application, and employed a world-class test description language to tie it all together.

So, *all* we have to do is finish writing those tests. In particular, we need to exercise the password dialog box that protects each document's contents. And we'll top things off by making sure that the program acts like the text editors people are used to—cut, paste, and all that.

We have a lot of ground to cover, but we also have a lot of good tools to help us—so I'm going to pick up the pace a bit. I may gloss over the details of the occasional low-level API call or omit a definition if it's similar to what we've seen before, but the full source code to the chapter is available in case you want to take a closer peek at the terrain we're racing through.

5.1 Save Me!

In previous chapters, we've been mostly concerned with the behavior and appearance of the main window. We've always canceled out of the Save dialog box. Let's change that.

The Spec

Imagine how you'd want the Save feature to work. You have a new document with no password, you click Save As, and you assign a password.

```
     describe 'Saving a document for the first time' do
       it 'requires a password' do
❶        note = Note.open
         note.save_as 'SavedNote', 'password'
         note.should have_prompted(:for_password)
❷        note.exit!
       end
     end
```

We'll be using that setup and teardown code at ❶ and ❷ in a lot of our examples, so we're going to add a RSpec-ful twist to put that common code in one place.

Learning to Share

In all the tests we've written so far, we create a new Note object at the beginning of each example, and we call the object's exit!() method afterward.

Wouldn't it be nice to have to type that code only once?

Enter our trio of champions: before, after, and :shared. These three features of RSpec help you reuse setup and teardown code across several examples. The custom is to put this common code into its own file, spec_helper.rb (don't forget to add require 'spec_helper' at the top of your spec!).

```
home_stretch/spec_helper.rb
```

```
❶  describe 'a new document', :shared => true do
❷    before do
       @note = Note.open
     end

❸    after do
❹      @note.exit! if @note.running?
     end
   end
```

Our common setup/teardown code is at ❷ and ❸. RSpec will run anything in a before or after block at the beginning or end of each example, respectively. Notice that @note has become an attribute, since it's now shared between the setup routine and the actual test code.

The :shared => true tag at ❶ tells RSpec that we're not going to run this describe block directly; instead, we're going to incorporate it into other describe blocks. We'll see how to do that in a minute.

See the bit about @note.running? at ❹? That will let us cavalierly write test code without regard to tidying up. Some examples will call exit!() themselves (if they're testing a specific way to leave the app), and others will just leave it to the cleanup code.

Here's what the implementation of running?() looks like inside LockNote:

`home_stretch/locknote.rb`

```
def running?
  @main_window.handle != 0 && is_window(@main_window.handle) != 0
end
```

IsWindow() is an API call that pretty much does what it says on the tin. The Ruby declaration for it is trivial, so we don't need to elaborate on it here.

And here's the JunqueNote version:

`home_stretch/junquenote.rb`

```
def running?
  @main_window && @main_window.visible
end
```

In order to use the shared setup/teardown code, we just put it_should_behave_like at the top of our describe block, like so:

`home_stretch/note_spec.rb`

```
describe 'Saving a document for the first time' do
  it_should_behave_like 'a new document'

  it 'requires a password' do
❶    @note.save_as 'MyNote'
❷    @note.should have_prompted(:for_password)
  end
end
```

At ❶, we're calling a new save_as() method that we're eventually going to have to implement; more on that in a sec.

But first, note that should have_prompted now has a parameter at ❷. Why is that?

As our script grows, we are going to have to track several kinds of prompts. In addition to the classic "are you sure you want to exit?" dialog box, we'll need to watch for a filename prompt, a password prompt, and so on.

The new implementation of has_prompted() is easy: we just have to
change the @prompted attribute from a Boolean to a hash:

home_stretch/note.rb

```
def has_prompted?(kind)
  @prompted[kind]
end
```

Any of the old specs that use should have_prompted will need to be
updated, as will the exit!() method. You'll also see (in Section 5.3, *Reini-
tializing initialize()*, on page 74) that initialize() sets @prompted to an empty
Hash.

Now, let's turn our attention to save_as().

Saving Flexibly

The basic mechanics of saving are pretty simple. We pick a filename
and then pick a password. But in most of our RSpec examples, we don't
care as much *what* the password is as we do *how* it's entered (for example, do we cancel or perhaps try a mismatched password/confirmation
pair?).

So, it makes sense for our script to assume that the password and confirmation will usually be, say, "password," and let individual examples
override these defaults. That's what the code at ❶ accomplishes in the
following excerpt:

home_stretch/note.rb

```
DefaultOptions = {
  :password => 'password',
  :confirmation => true
}

def save_as(name, with_options = {})
❶    options = DefaultOptions.merge with_options

❷    @path = @@app.path_to(name)
     File.delete @path if File.exist? @path

❸    menu 'File', 'Save As...'

❹    enter_filename @path
     assign_password options
end
```

Notice that save_as() doesn't take a full path; it just takes a document
name. At ❷, we transform one into the other by adding a directory and

an extension.[1] That keeps potentially changing information such as file extensions and absolute paths out of our top-level test code.

All the real work happens in enter_filename() and assign_password() at ❹. enter_filename() is worth taking a look at here:

`home_stretch/note.rb`

```
def enter_filename(path, approval = '_Save')
❶   dialog(@@titles[:file]) do |d|
      d.type_in path
      d.click approval
    end
end
```

assign_password() will have to wait for now; passwords are a big enough topic for their own section. All we need to do for now is trust that it'll wait for the password prompt, do the typing for us, and fill in the relevant parts of @prompted with true or false values.

At ❸, we're doing a bit of multiplatform magic to make menus work the same in both LockNote and JunqueNote. We want that call to translate to something like this on Windows:

```
WM_COMMAND = 0x0111
```

```
@main_window.post_message WM_COMMAND, ID_FILE_SAVE_AS, 0
```

...and this in JRuby:

```
@main_window.push_menu_no_block 'File|Save As...', '|'
```

Let's look at the JRuby translation first. All we have to do is paste that line of code into a function definition and change the hard-coded menu item into a parameter.

Actually, we want to parameterize the *kind* of menu too, not just the name. Instead of always calling push_menu_no_block(), we would like to choose push_menu() or push_menu_no_block(), based on whether the script is supposed to block waiting for the action to complete:

`home_stretch/junquenote.rb`

```
def menu(name, item, wait = false)
  action = wait ? :push_menu : :push_menu_no_block
  @menu_bar.send action,  name + '|' + item, '|'
end
```

---

1. LockNote saves its documents as self-decoding .exes, while JunqueNote uses its own extension.

> ## Joe Asks...
> ### What's with the New send_message()?
>
> So, you've noticed that the fourth parameter of send_message()
> has changed from a string pointer to a plain ol' integer? Good
> eye.
>
> Different Windows messages have different interpretations of
> that last value. And we'll be using it as an integer much more
> often than as a buffer. So, we've changed it. The old version is
> still around, but it's now called send_with_buffer().

Now, let's look at the Windows equivalent. We need to get from 'File',
'Save As...' to the equivalent C constant name, ID_FILE_SAVE_AS or ID_FILE_
SAVEAS (different apps use different underscoring conventions):

`home_stretch/locknote.rb`

```
def menu(name, item, wait = false)
  multiple_words = /[.]/
  single_word = /[ .]/

  [multiple_words, single_word].each do |pattern|
    words = item.gsub(pattern, '').split
    const_name = ['ID', name, *words].join('_').upcase
    msg = WM_COMMAND

    begin
      id = LockNote.const_get const_name
      action = wait ? :send_message : :post_message

      return send(action, @main_window.handle, msg, id, 0)
    rescue NameError
    end
  end
end
```

The only thing remaining is to figure out how we get C names like
ID_FILE_SAVE_AS into Ruby in the first place. JRuby folks, we'll see you
after the next section.

Is It C, or Is It Ruby?

On Windows, we might be tempted to hard-code the integer value of
each menu ID, but there's a better solution.

LockNote's developers have gone to all the trouble of providing C header files containing their menu IDs. Why duplicate that effort? WindowsGui can be taught to read these definitions directly from the C source code:

`home_stretch/windows_gui.rb`

```
def self.load_symbols(header)
  File.open(header) do |f|
    f.grep(/#define\s+(ID\w+)\s+(\w+)/) do
      name = $1
❶     value = (0 == $2.to_i) ? $2.hex : $2.to_i
❷     WindowsGui.const_set name, value
    end
  end
end
```

All we have to do is look through a header file for #define statements, figure out whether a given definition is decimal or hex at ❶, and dynamically assign the constant at ❷.

And we use it like this:

`home_stretch/locknote.rb`

```
BasePath = "C:\\LockNote"
WindowsGui.load_symbols "#{BasePath}\\src\\resource.h"
WindowsGui.load_symbols "#{BasePath}\\src\\atlres.h"
ID_HELP_ABOUT = ID_APP_ABOUT
```

I'm fudging a little bit here. The second file, atlres.h, doesn't come with LockNote—it's part of the Windows Template Library. The exact path will depend on WTL's version number and where it's installed. You'll either need to modify the test script to point to your copy of WTL or just grab a version of atlres.h online and put it in LockNote's src directory.[2]

One last thing: you'll see that I've added an alias for the one menu command that doesn't fit the ID_*menu_item* pattern.

OK, enough about the menu. Let's tackle those prompts.

5.2 The Password Is...

There are three different situations where we need to enter a password in LockNote:

- In order to open a saved document, we enter its password once to unlock it.

---

2. http://wtl.cvs.sf.net/wtl/wtl/include/atlres.h

- When we save a document for the first time, we enter its password twice.

- When we change a password, we have to enter the old one once and the new one twice.

The Three Flavors

Let's look at the simplest case first:

`home_stretch/note.rb`

```ruby
def unlock_password(with_options = {})
  options = DefaultOptions.merge with_options
❶ options[:confirmation] = false

  enter_password options
  watch_for_error
end
```

To unlock an existing document, we need to enter the password only once. So at ❶, we forcibly set :confirmation to false. That's the signal to our password entry function (which we'll define soon) to skip the confirmation step.

When we're *saving* a document, the picture is a little more complicated. If there's an error message (that is, if the password and confirmation don't match), we end up back in the password prompt. Our new function reflects this difference at ❶:

`home_stretch/note.rb`

```ruby
def assign_password(with_options = {})
  options = DefaultOptions.merge with_options

  enter_password options
  watch_for_error

  if @prompted[:with_error]
❶   enter_password :cancel_password => true
  end
end
```

Changing a password is the most complicated case of the three, but we can think of it as just a single-entry "unlock document" dialog box, followed by a double-entry "assign password" dialog box. The only thing different is how we handle the options passed in.

home_stretch/note.rb

```
def change_password(with_options = {})
  old_options = {
①   :password => with_options[:old_password]}

  new_options = {
    :password => with_options[:password],
    :confirmation =>
      with_options[:confirmation] ||
②     with_options[:password]}

  menu 'File', 'Change Password...'

  unlock_password old_options
  assign_password new_options
end
```

There seems to be a lot of option juggling at ❶ and ❷. But it's all for a good cause.

We don't want to require our top-level test script to have to trail a mile of parameters off the end of change_password(), like this:

```
@locknote.change_password \
  :old_password => 'password',
  :old_confirmation => false,
  :password => 'new',
  :confirmation => 'new'
```

Yuck! The previous option code will let us reduce that to the following:

```
@locknote.change_password \
  :old_password => 'password',
  :password => 'new'
```

That's much better. Now all we have to do is define the two utility functions shared by these three password entry methods.

No Surprises

The implementation of enter_password() contains no surprises at all.[3] First, let's see the LockNote way.

---

3. The Windows version has a couple new constants, though—see Section A.4, *A Few Win32 Definitions*, on page 170 for their definitions.

`home_stretch/locknote.rb`

```ruby
def enter_password(with_options = {})
  options = DefaultOptions.merge with_options

  @prompted[:for_password] = dialog(@@titles[:dialog]) do |d|
    type_in options[:password]

    confirmation =
      options[:confirmation] == true ?
      options[:password] :
      options[:confirmation]

    if confirmation
      keystroke VK_TAB
      type_in confirmation
    end

    d.click options[:cancel_password] ? IDCANCEL : IDOK
  end
end
```

And now, here's JunqueNote's version:

`home_stretch/junquenote.rb`

```ruby
def enter_password(with_options = {})
  options = DefaultOptions.merge with_options

  @prompted[:for_password] = single_password_entry \
    options[:password], options[:cancel_password]

  confirmation =
    options[:confirmation] == true ?
    options[:password] :
    options[:confirmation]

  if @prompted[:for_password] && confirmation
    single_password_entry confirmation, false
  end
end

def single_password_entry(password, cancel)
  dialog('Input') do |d|
    d.type_in password
    d.click(cancel ? 'Cancel' : 'OK')
  end
end
```

In case the password entry fails, we'll need to watch for errors.

Here's how to do that in LockNote:

`home_stretch/locknote.rb`

```
ErrorIcon = 0x0014

def watch_for_error
  if @prompted[:for_password]
    @prompted[:with_error] = dialog(@@titles[:dialog]) do |d|
      d.click IDCANCEL if get_dlg_item(d.handle, ErrorIcon) > 0
    end
  end
end
```

❶

There's just one subtle point here. In LockNote, as in most Windows apps, nearly all dialog boxes have the same title. So, the only way to know we're inside an error dialog box—and not, say, in a password dialog box—is to look for the little exclamation mark icon.

If the test at ❶ passes, we've found an error dialog box, and the dialog() method we wrote in Section 4.2, *Pain-Free Windows*, on page 51 will dismiss it automatically.

If, on the other hand, the error icon *isn't* there, the expression has a value of nil, which accomplishes two things for us:

- @prompted[:with_error] will also be assigned a value of nil, meaning "we didn't see an error prompt."

- We're implicitly telling dialog() *not* to dismiss the window. We need to leave it onscreen, because no doubt some other piece of code is expecting to see it.

JunqueNote doesn't need any icon-spotting code, since its error dialog box has a distinct title. Accordingly, its watch_for_error() method will be a little simpler:

`home_stretch/junquenote.rb`

```
def watch_for_error
  if @prompted[:for_password]
    @prompted[:with_error] = dialog('Oops') do |d|
      d.click 'OK'
    end
  end
end
```

Got all that? Good! It's time to put our password code to use.

5.3   Document Wrangling

We should now feel confident that we can handle any type of password dialog box that either LockNote or JunqueNote throws at us. So, let's wade on in to some cross-platform test cases.

Password Special Cases

We have test code that can assign a password and save a document to disk. Let's take care of a couple of special cases around passwords. If we try to save a document but cancel or mistype the password, the app should skip saving the file:

`home_stretch/note_spec.rb`

```
describe 'The password assignment prompt' do
  it_should_behave_like 'a new document'

  it 'ignores the new password if cancelled' do
    @note.text = 'changed'
    @note.save_as 'MyNote', :cancel_password => true
    @note.exit!
❶    @note.should have_prompted(:to_confirm_exit)
  end

  it 'ignores an unconfirmed password' do
    @note.text = 'changed'
    @note.save_as 'SavedNote', :confirmation => 'mismatch'
    @note.should have_prompted(:with_error)
    @note.exit!
❷    @note.should have_prompted(:to_confirm_exit)
  end
end
```

How do we know that the file never got saved? Because the next time we try to exit, it asks us whether we want to save. We watch for this condition at ❶ and ❷.

Grand Reopening

Let's move on to the prompt that greets us when we reopen a saved document:

`home_stretch/note_spec.rb`

```
describe 'The password entry prompt' do
❶  it_should_behave_like 'a saved document'

  it 'ignores the password if cancelled' do
    note = Note.open 'SavedNote', :cancel_password => true
    note.should_not be_running
  end
```

```
  it 'exits with an error message for an invalid password' do
    note = Note.open 'SavedNote', :password => 'invalid'
    note.should_not be_running
    note.should have_prompted(:with_error)
  end
end
```

As you can see at ❶, this test uses a new shared behavior, called "a saved document." Its job is to make sure we have an example of a saved note in place before our test starts:

`home_stretch/spec_helper.rb`

```
describe 'a saved document', :shared => true do
  before do
❶   Note.fixture 'SavedNote'
  end
end
```

The fixture() method at ❶ is responsible for preparing a saved file. We could generate one from the GUI every time we run our tests, but it's much faster to use a prefab one that we build by hand.

A Permanent Fixture

So, let's put that sample file together.

Launch LockNote or JunqueNote manually from where you installed it, and save a new document called SavedNoteFixture with the creative choice of "password" as the password.[4] Then, add the following class-level method to Note():

`home_stretch/note.rb`

```
require 'fileutils'

class Note
  def self.fixture(name)
    source = @@app.path_to(name + 'Fixture')
    target = @@app.path_to(name)

    FileUtils.rm target if File.exist? target
    FileUtils.copy source, target
  end
end
```

Now, our script will always have a fresh copy of its test fixture in place. The two path_to() implementations aren't worth showing here; they just wrap the fixture name with the appropriate directory and extension.

---

4. I have the same combination on my luggage!

Reinitializing initialize()

We'll need to add a couple of parameters to LockNote's initialize() method
to allow us to start the application with a saved file instead of a "Welcome to the app" message.

home_stretch/locknote.rb

```ruby
def initialize(name = 'LockNote', with_options = {})
  options = DefaultOptions.merge(with_options)

  @prompted = {}
  @path = LockNote.path_to(name)

  system 'start "" "' + @path + '"'
  unlock_password options

  if @prompted[:with_error] || options[:cancel_password]
    @main_window = Window.new 0
    sleep 1.0
  else
    @main_window = Window.top_level "#{name} - Steganos LockNote"
    @edit_window = @main_window.child "ATL:00434310"

    set_foreground_window @main_window.handle
  end
end
```

The method has gotten a little bigger, but it's all just pieces we've built
up over the course of the chapter. JunqueNote gets a similar treatment:

home_stretch/junquenote.rb

```ruby
def initialize(name = nil, with_options = {})
  options = DefaultOptions.merge(with_options)

  @prompted = {}
  @path = JunqueNote.path_to(name) if name

  @program = JunqueNoteApp.new
  @main_window = JFrameOperator.new 'JunqueNote'
  @edit_window = JTextAreaOperator.new @main_window
  @menu_bar = JMenuBarOperator.new @main_window

  if name
    menu 'File', 'Open...'
    enter_filename @path, '_Open'
    unlock_password options
  end

  if @prompted[:with_error] || options[:cancel_password]
    @program = nil
  end
end
```

Unlike a LockNote file, a saved JunqueNote document is not self-decrypting; we have to trigger the Open menu item ourselves.

Last Night's Notes

Just one more set of examples on the subject of document management and then we can move on to text editor stuff such as cutting and pasting.

We've dealt with the act of saving files. And we've dealt with how to reopen them. Now, we need to look at how a document behaves *after* we've reopened it:

`home_stretch/note_spec.rb`

```
describe 'A previously saved document' do
  it_should_behave_like 'a saved document'
❶  it_should_behave_like 'a reopened document'

  it 'preserves and encrypts the contents of the file' do
    @note.text.should include('Welcome')
❷    IO.read(@note.path).should_not include('Welcome')
  end

  it 'does not require a password on subsequent saves' do
    @note.text = 'changed'
❸    @note.exit! :save_as => 'MyNote'
    @note.should_not have_prompted(:for_password)
  end

  it 'supports changing the password' do
    @note.change_password \
      :old_password => 'password',
      :password => 'new'
    @note.exit!

    @note = Note.open 'SavedNote', :password => 'new'
    @note.should_not have_prompted(:with_error)
    @note.should be_running
  end
end
```

Notice at ❶ that we're piling multiple it_should_behave_like expressions on top of each other. RSpec does what you'd expect here: it runs the before and after blocks in the order that you list the shared behaviors.

Speaking of shared behavior, we're using a new one here called "a reopened document." It's just like "a new document" that we defined in Section 5.1, *Learning to Share*, on page 62, except that now we're starting with an existing file called SavedNote instead of a new file.

The line at ❷ merits a closer look. We want to make sure that LockNote and JunqueNote are scrambling their on-disk files to protect them from prying eyes. So, as a quick check, we look at the entire contents of the file for a sample word from the text.

And how did we get the document's full path so we could read the file? By making path a read-only attribute of the Note class.

At ❸, we see that exit!() will need a new parameter so that we can indicate when we want to save on exiting, instead of just blowing past the confirmation dialog box.

Here's the new, more flexible version of the exit!() method:

home_stretch/note.rb

```
def exit!(with_options = {})
  options = DefaultOptions.merge with_options

  @main_window.close

  @prompted[:to_confirm_exit] = dialog(@@titles[:exit]) do |d|
    d.click(options[:save_as] ? '_Yes' : '_No')
  end

  if options[:save_as]
    path = @@app.path_to options[:save_as]
    enter_filename path
    assign_password options
  end
end
```

As with initialize(), you can see that exit!() is built on the simple dialog box and utility functions we've put together throughout this chapter.

5.4   Cut to the Paste

We have been talking about documents and passwords for so long that it's easy to forget that there are text-editing features we need to test as well.

The Undo That You Do

Folks using LockNote and JunqueNote will expect to find all the standard text-editing features they're used to: Undo, Cut, Copy, Paste, and so forth.

Let's put together a few simple examples of how these should work:

`home_stretch/note_spec.rb`

```ruby
describe 'The editor' do
  it_should_behave_like 'a new document'

  it 'supports multiple levels of undo' do
    @note.text = 'abc'

    @note.undo
    @note.text.should == 'ab'

    @note.undo
    @note.text.should == 'a'
  end

  it 'supports copying and pasting text' do
    @note.text = 'itchy'
    @note.select_all
    @note.copy
    @note.text.should == 'itchy'

    @note.text = 'scratchy'
    @note.select_all
    @note.paste
    @note.text.should == 'itchy'
  end

  it 'supports cutting and pasting text' do
    @note.text = 'pineapple'
    @note.select_all
    @note.cut
    @note.text.should be_empty

    @note.text = 'mango'
    @note.select_all
    @note.paste
    @note.text.should == 'pineapple'
  end
end
```

We've introduced several new methods here: undo(), select_all(), cut(), copy(), and paste(). Their implementations will all follow the same pattern:

```ruby
def some_function
  menu 'Edit', 'Some Function'
end
```

Of course, Ruby can and should write those functions for us.

```
home_stretch/note.rb
```

```ruby
[:undo, :cut, :copy, :paste, :find_next].each do |method|
  item = method.to_s.split('_').collect {|m| m.capitalize}.join(' ')
❶ define_method(method) {menu 'Edit', item, :wait}
end
```

Notice the :wait at ❶? This signals that the script should wait at that
spot until the app has finished carrying out the Undo, or Paste, or
whatever it's working on. As long as you're sure that the task will take
only, say, a couple tenths of a second to complete, this is usually a
reasonable approach. You may want to add a timeout in case the app
hangs, though.

Blocking on a menu event like this wouldn't work for something that
required a lengthy user interaction, like Save As or Find. Whatever code
you'd written to deal with dialog boxes and buttons would never run,
because you'd be waiting forever in your menu function.

Searching for a Replacement

Now that we have a handle on Undo and Cut/Paste, let's move on to
text searching. With the few examples we have, it wouldn't be such a
bad thing to hard-code our search term into our spec. But it would be
mildly annoying if we later decided—as I did while writing this book—to
switch to a different sample sentence and had to manually recalculate
where all the matches occur. ("Let's see, the second occurrence of the
word *fox* happens at the 16th character. . . .")

So, let's set up a new shared behavior and calculate our search matches
using regular expressions for case matching, multiple occurrences, and
so on:

```
home_stretch/spec_helper.rb
```

```ruby
describe 'a searchable document', :shared => true do
  before do
    @example = 'The longest island is Isabel Island.'
    @term = 'Is'

    @first_match = @example.index(/Is/i)
    @second_match = @example.index(/Is/i, @first_match + 1)
    @reverse_match = @example.rindex(/Is/i)
    @word_match = @example.index(/Is\b/i)
    @case_match = @example.index(/Is/)

    @note.text = @example
  end
end
```

Now, writing the actual examples is a snap:

`home_stretch/note_spec.rb`

```ruby
describe 'The Find window' do
  it_should_behave_like 'a new document'
  it_should_behave_like 'a searchable document'

  it 'supports searching forward' do
    @note.go_to :beginning
    @note.find @term
    @note.selection.begin.should == @first_match

    @note.find_next
    @note.selection.begin.should == @second_match
  end

  it 'supports searching backward' do
    @note.go_to :end
    @note.find @term, :direction => :back
    @note.selection.begin.should == @reverse_match
  end

  it 'can restrict its search to whole words' do
    pending 'on hold' do
      @note.go_to :beginning
      @note.find @term, :whole_word => true
      @note.selection.begin.should == @word_match
    end
  end

  it 'can restrict its search to exact case matches' do
    @note.go_to :beginning
    @note.find @term, :exact_case => true
    @note.selection.begin.should == @case_match
  end
end
```

❶

What's with the new pending tag at ❶? Neither LockNote nor Jun-queNote has implemented whole-word matching yet, so we wrap the test in a pending block.

When a future version of either app comes along and implements this feature, our test reports will switch from saying, "This feature is pending," to complaining, "You said this feature was absent, but it's there now!" That will be our clue to revisit our test script.

The cornerstone of the search tests is the find() method we're going to add to LockNote. . .

home_stretch/locknote.rb

```ruby
WholeWord = 0x0410
ExactCase = 0x0411
SearchUp  = 0x0420

def find(term, with_options={})
  menu 'Edit', 'Find...'

  appeared = dialog('Find') do |d|
    type_in term

    d.click WholeWord if with_options[:whole_word]
    d.click ExactCase if with_options[:exact_case]
    d.click SearchUp if :back == with_options[:direction]

    d.click IDOK
    d.click IDCANCEL
  end

  raise 'Find dialog did not appear' unless appeared
end
```

and to JunqueNote:

home_stretch/junquenote.rb

```ruby
def find(term, with_options={})
  command = 'Find...'
  command = 'Find Exact Case...' if with_options[:exact_case]
  command = 'Reverse ' + command if :back == with_options[:direction]

  menu 'Edit', command

  dialog('Input') do |d|
    d.type_in term
    d.click 'OK'
  end
end
```

After we've performed the search, we need to figure out whether we found anything. The Find feature highlights the next match, so on Windows, all we need to do is send the EM_GETSEL message to the text window and do a little byte arithmetic:

home_stretch/locknote.rb

```ruby
def selection
  result = send_message @edit_window.handle, EM_GETSEL, 0, 0
  bounds = [result].pack('L').unpack('SS')
❶ bounds[0]...bounds[1]
end
```

Since a text selection spans a range of characters, it makes sense to return a Ruby Range object from selection(), as we do at ❶ (notice the three dots marking this Range's excluded endpoint).

In JRuby, we just use Jemmy's getSelectionStart() and getSelectionEnd() methods:

`home_stretch/junquenote.rb`

```ruby
def selection
  first = @edit_window.get_selection_start
  last = @edit_window.get_selection_end
  Range.new(first, last - 1)
end
```

Finally, we need a way to jump around in the document so that we can go to the end and search backward. For the coarse-grained control of jumping from one end of the document to the other, we can just rely on keyboard commands in Windows. . .

`home_stretch/locknote.rb`

```ruby
def go_to(where)
  case where
    when :beginning
      keystroke VK_CONTROL, VK_HOME
    when :end
      keystroke VK_CONTROL, VK_END
  end
end
```

or JTextArea built-ins in JRuby:

`home_stretch/junquenote.rb`

```ruby
def go_to(where)
  case where
    when :beginning
      @edit_window.set_caret_position 0
    when :end
      @edit_window.set_caret_position text.length
  end
end
```

That's enough for us to do some basic text searches. We could try combining, say, a backward search with case matching. Doing so wouldn't really illuminate the process of writing examples, so let's move on.

5.5 Are We There Yet?

Wow. Let's just take a step back and exult in what we've accomplished. In less than 200 lines of test code, we've touched every feature of our application.

What's more, we've created a test script that we could hand to any nondeveloper—a documentation writer, a manager, or, in my case, a long-suffering spouse—and they would get the gist of how the program works. So, are we done?

Well, there are still a couple of minor things we haven't covered. I didn't show you the code that hits the About menu item and watches for a simple help dialog box. But you could write that code in your sleep.[5] And we could, if we wanted, use the shared-behavior technique to streamline the previous chapter's code.

But I suspect that's too literal of an answer. After all, we've exercised the app pretty well from a sketchy, cocktail-napkin perspective. You're probably wondering, "Can we *please* stop writing test code now?"

You could. But you'd miss out on the best part.

We're nearing the limit of what these simple tests will do for us. How do we catch things like memory leaks, buffer overflows, and weird glitches that happen only on certain kinds of input?

There's a huge colossal world of scripted testing techniques out there. Let's go take a peek.

---

5. I *am* writing it in my sleep. It's 2:15 a.m. here; if I can do it, you can do it.

Part II

Aspects of Testing

Chapter 6

Branching Out

We've spent the first half of this book building up a series of test scripts for a real-world app. What do we have to show for it?[1] Two things.

6.1 Testing the App

First, we now have a simple automated test for the program's GUI. We can use it like a crude floodlight to spot the most severe regressions cheaply. It's not going to catch the kind of subtle, weird bugs you see only by actually interacting with the app (in other words, most bugs).

But our script can do at least one thing a manual test can't: it can run after every build as a quick "go or no-go" indicator. If a developer checks in a code change that screws up the app badly enough to fail this suite, the build will probably be of too poor quality to bother testing manually.

6.2 Testing the Tests

Another point that's easy to miss: we've exercised our test framework itself. The process of writing that Note class and throwing it up against the app over and over and over again shook out lots of issues with our own test code.

By working out the finer points of timing, character sets, dialog boxes, and so on, we've gained some measure of confidence in the building

---

1. Aside from the warm, fuzzy feeling of having created a specification out of running code, I mean.

blocks of our tests.[2] That'll become important as we assemble these blocks into more complicated setups in the later chapters.

So when we put together an overnight stress test that includes something like this...

```
note.text = punishingly_huge_random_text
note.cut
note.paste
# ...
```

we'll have a good idea that the underlying GUI code will drive our app appropriately.

6.3 Putting the Pieces Together

A quick acceptance test and a warm feeling about being an integral part of the development process are nice. But what about catching some bugs?

Now that we know how to find windows and controls, type keystrokes, and click buttons, how might we combine these steps in ways that help us find and remove errors from the application?

Here are a few ideas:

- Run a loop that opens, modifies, and saves a document all night while watching the app's memory usage to try to catch resource leaks.

- To unearth buffer overruns, open every dialog box in the app and flood each text control with extra-long strings, illegal characters (for example, filenames with pipes), embedded NUL bytes, huge numbers, and so on.

- Barrage the main window of the app with random keystrokes and clicks for a few hours, trying to trip it up somehow.

- Repeat a complicated series of steps in order to trigger an intermittent bug that happens only under very specific conditions.

- Try dozens or hundreds of different combinations of input data.

Over the next few chapters, we are going to look at some of these techniques.

---

2. See the Heckle (http://seattlerb.rubyforge.org) and rcov (http://eigenclass.org/hiki.rb?rcov) projects for examples of how we can quantify this confidence.

6.4 Moving On

Where the first half of the book was a depth-first look at scripting one application, this half will be a broader survey of GUI testing topics. The level of detail will be a little lighter. We'll look at a few different test techniques and at how to test on a couple more app platforms.

The examples won't be "bilingual" anymore, and they won't always be confined to LockNote (though we will look at it for a couple more tests).

We're going to start gradually by injecting bits of random behavior into the scripts we wrote for Part I. By the time we've reached the end of Chapter 7, *Keep 'Em Guessing: Introducing Randomness*, on page 89, we'll have departed from our clean RSpec aesthetic and created a punishing test monkey to bash on the GUI.

From there, it's on to Chapter 8, *Turn the Tables: Matrix Testing*, on page 101, where we'll explore data-driven testing. When you cut nearly all the boilerplate and programmer-speak out of your tests, you're left with just the data in a clean, tabular format.

In Chapter 9, *Testing the Tubes: Web Applications*, on page 115, we'll look at web testing toolkits and techniques. As with desktop apps, keep an eye out for ways to keep the mechanics of buttons and clicks from cluttering up the language of our tests.

Some situations demand longer, more involved scripts. In Chapter 10, *Testing in Plain English: Story Runner*, on page 137, we'll see how to weave our tests into an overarching, plain-language narrative.

Finally, to cleanse the palate, we'll have a bit of fun on the Mac desktop in Chapter 11, *One More Thing: Testing on the Mac*, on page 157.

Ready to get started?

## Chapter 7

Keep 'Em Guessing: Introducing Randomness

All right, no more Mr. Nice Tester. We've been coddling our application, gently running our test scripts the same way each time. That was fine for documenting our expectations of the app and getting our test framework up to speed.

But there could be dozens of bugs lurking in the program, waiting to be exposed if we'd only just do things with a little different order or timing. Let's try to trip up the app with a little randomness.

7.1 Keys, Menu, or Mouse?

In all our previous tests, we always exercise each feature the same way. For example, we always paste text by selecting the Paste item from the Edit menu. But there are at least two other ways to paste: pressing `Ctrl+V` and using the right-click menu.

What if there were some weird interaction that caused problems with text manipulation, but only under certain unusual circumstances involving the keyboard? A lot of bugs are like that. If your test script always uses the menu, you'll never catch it.[1]

---

1. Your manual tests *might* catch it, if you don't treat them like a rote "try all the menus" exercise.

Keeping Things Interesting

Why not teach our script to act a bit differently each time? Let's start small with a single feature—Paste, for instance. Each time the test script calls paste(), we'll decide based on a random number whether to use the menu bar, keyboard, or context (right-click) menu:

`guessing/locknote.rb`

```
        srand
❶       $seed ||= srand
        srand $seed
        puts "Using random seed #{$seed}"

        class LockNote
          def paste
            case rand(3)
            when 0
              menu 'Edit', 'Paste'
              puts 'Pasting from the menu'
            when 1
              keystroke VK_CONTROL, ?V
              puts 'Pasting from a keyboard shortcut'
            when 2
❷            @main_window.click EditControl, :right
              type_in 'P'
              puts 'Pasting from a context menu'
            end
          end
        end
```

At ❷, we've added a new parameter to Window#click() to let us specify which mouse button we want to use. As in previous chapters, we identify the edit area by its window class. (EditControl is just a constant assigned to that hard-to-remember 'ATL:something' name.)

If we add code like this to some of our other functions, our test script will behave a little more like a real user: sometimes it'll use the mouse and sometimes the keyboard.

There is one potential downside to changing things up on each run like this. If your test happens to find a bug in the app, you might have trouble repeating the problem on the next run.

That's why it's important to record the value you use to seed Ruby's pseudorandom number generator, as we have at ❶. Because srand() returns the *previous* seed value, it takes three calls to the function to get what we want.

Now, if we need to "play back" a particular sequence, we can put the seed we want in an external file, say, seed.rb...

guessing/seed.rb

```
$seed = 12345
```

and use it like this:

```
C:\> spec -rseed -rlocknote -fs note_spec.rb
```

Adding that case/when code to every action that we want to randomize is going to get old really fast. Let's think about a way to avoid that kind of duplication.

Action!

What we're really doing in that case structure is defining all the different ways the Paste action could be carried out. Other actions in our software (Exit, Undo, Find) also have multiple ways for the user to perform them.

It makes sense to teach our test library the notion of defining an action, so we can do something like this:

guessing/locknote.rb

```
def_action :paste,
  :menu => ['Edit', 'Paste', :wait],
  :keyboard => [VK_CONTROL, ?V],
  :context => 'p'
```

The body of def_action() is just our Paste example from earlier, made more general:

guessing/locknote.rb

```
class LockNote
  @@default_way = :random

  def self.def_action(name, options, way = nil)
    define_method name do
      keys = options.keys.sort {|k| k.to_s}

      way ||= @@default_way
      key = case way
        when nil;    keys.last
        when :random; keys[rand(keys.size)]
        else         way
      end

      action = options[key]
```

```
        case key
        when :menu
          menu *action
          puts "Performing #{name} from the menu bar"

        when :keyboard
          keystroke *action
          sleep 0.5
          puts "Performing #{name} from a keyboard shortcut"

        when :context
          @main_window.click LockNote::EditControl, :right
          sleep 0.5
          type_in action
          sleep 0.5
          puts "Performing #{name} from a context menu"

        else
          raise "Don't know how to use #{key}"
        end
      end
    end
end
```

Notice how, at ❶, we've turned the preferred type of action into what amounts to a configuration setting. You could use :random for overnight stress testing, :keyboard to run a few tests on a mouse-free machine, or something else (e.g., :preferred) for times when you need predictability.

Equipped with this class-level method, we can define several common GUI actions:

`guessing/locknote.rb`

```
def_action :undo,
  :menu => ['Edit', 'Undo', :wait],
  :keyboard => [VK_CONTROL, ?Z]

def_action :cut,
  :menu => ['Edit', 'Cut', :wait],
  :keyboard => [VK_CONTROL, ?X],
  :context => 't'

def_action :copy,
  :menu => ['Edit', 'Copy', :wait],
  :keyboard => [VK_CONTROL, ?C],
  :context => 'c'

def_action :delete,
  :keyboard => [VK_BACK],
  :context => 'd'
```

```
def_action :select_all,
  :menu => ['Edit', 'Select All', :wait],
  :keyboard => [VK_CONTROL, ?A],
  :context => 'a'
```

Our script has just been given a bit more bug-finding potency, but it's also more expressive now. It almost reads like documentation: "The Undo action can be triggered from the Edit > Undo menu or the `Ctrl+Z` keystroke."

Decluttering

Although our test library has become more readable, our test report has become a mess:

```
Using random seed 12345

The editor
Performing select_all from the menu bar
Performing delete from a keyboard shortcut
Performing select_all from a keyboard shortcut
Performing cut from a keyboard shortcut
Performing select_all from a context menu
Performing delete from a keyboard shortcut
Performing select_all from the menu bar
Performing paste from the menu bar
- supports cutting and pasting text

Finished in 13.809 seconds

1 example, 0 failures
```

Let's use Ruby's logging library so we can separate the test report from the extra info:

guessing/locknote.rb

```
require 'logger'

❶ class SimpleFormatter < Logger::Formatter
    def call(severity, time, progname, msg)
      msg2str(msg) + "\n"
    end
  end

  $logger = Logger.new STDERR
❷ $logger.formatter = SimpleFormatter.new
```

Logger's default format is pretty verbose: it includes a time stamp, a logging level, and so on. At ❶ and ❷, we've trimmed it to just a simple description.

Now, if we replace all our calls to puts(), like this one. . .

```
puts "Performing #{name} from the menu bar"
```

with calls to $logger.info(), like this. . .

```
$logger.info "Performing #{name} from the menu bar"
```

then all the extra information not part of the test report will be directed to wherever the Logger is pointed, in this case STDERR. On Windows, you can redirect standard error to a file with the 2> operator:

```
C:\> spec -rlocknote -fs note_spec.rb 2>actions.txt
```

If one of our tests suddenly fails in the face of randomness, we now have the random number seed to re-create it and a detailed record of GUI actions to help us diagnose it.

7.2 Adding Lorem Ipsum to the Mix

Lorem Ipsum refers to a collection of random-looking pseudo-Latin text used by typographers for centuries as filler. In this section, we're going to feed LockNote this and other kinds of random text.

Why? Well, back when we were just documenting requirements, using the same example text each time was fine. But that's not going to cut it for bug hunting. If the app we're testing has some kind of error that shows up only with certain text—accented characters, long documents, or something like that—we'd like to increase our chances of finding it.

Line Noise

It'd be pretty easy to generate a brutal sequence of random printable and nonprintable ASCII characters, something like this:

```
def random_characters(length)
  (1..length).collect {rand 256}.pack 'C*'
end
```

You absolutely should test your document-handling code with text like this, but the GUI might not be the easiest place to do so. After all, if your random string contains NUL or vertical-tab characters, you probably won't be able to type them in.

So, assuming you're taking care of the truly untypeable examples in your non-GUI tests, let's narrow our focus to strings we can enter from the GUI. Just for fun, we'll throw in some UTF-8-encoded international characters, too, using Ruby's included jcode library.

```
require 'jcode'
$KCODE = 'U'

AsciiStart = 0x20
LatinStart = 0xA1

def random_characters(length)
  codes = (1..length).collect do
    start = (rand(2) == 0) ? AsciiStart : LatinStart
    start + rand(95)
  end

  codes.pack 'U*'
end
```

You might want to draw your random characters from a bigger pool than this fairly small Latin set. You'll need to define the virtual key codes for each character your script might need to type: punctuation, accented characters, and so on. The exact keystrokes will depend heavily on your keyboard layout.

Readable Text

The previous methods will generate strings that look like line noise. You'll probably also want to be able to generate "saner" strings that will be legible when they show up in your result logs. Just for fun, let's use a pseudorandom Lorem Ipsum text generator from the Internet.

Ruby's built-in open-uri library allows us to fetch text from websites pretty easily:

```
require 'open-uri'
doc = open 'http://www.lipsum.com/feed/html'
```

The result is a big chunk of HTML, with plenty of angle brackets for everyone. We need to drill down to the part that actually has the generated text in it:

```
<div id="lipsum">
  <p>
    Lorem ipsum dolor sit amet,...
  </p>
  ...
</div>
```

We could grab the words with a set of clever-enough regular expressions, but there's an easier way. The Hpricot library provides an easy way to parse HTML.

You can install it like this. . .

C:\> **gem install hpricot**

and use it like so:

guessing/spec_helper.rb

```ruby
require 'rubygems'
require 'hpricot'
require 'open-uri'

module RandomHelper
  def random_paragraph
    doc = Hpricot open('http://www.lipsum.com/feed/html?amount=1')
❶   (doc/"div#lipsum p").inner_html.strip
  end
end
```

The string div#lipsum p at ❶ is an XPath expression meaning "a paragraph inside the div whose id is lipsum."[2]

To use random_paragraph() in our RSpec tests, all we need to do is include the helper class, as we have at ❶ in this code:

guessing/spec_helper.rb

```ruby
describe 'a searchable document', :shared => true do
❶   include RandomHelper

    before do
❷     @example = random_paragraph

      words = @example.split /[^A-Za-z]+/
      last_cap = words.select {|w| w =~ /^[A-Z]/}.last
❸     @term = last_cap[0..1]

      @first_match = @example.index(/#{@term}/i)
      @second_match = @first_match ?
        @example.index(/#{@term}/i, @first_match + 1) :
        nil
      @reverse_match = @example.rindex(/#{@term}/i)
      @word_match = @example.index(/#{@term}\b/i)
      @case_match = @example.index(/#{@term}/)

      @note.text = @example
    end
end
```

---

2. We'll talk more about picking apart HTML documents with XPath in Chapter 9, *Testing the Tubes: Web Applications*, on page 115.

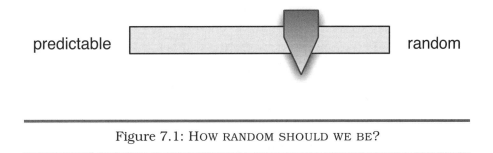

Figure 7.1: How random should we be?

Then, we replace the formerly hard-coded text at ❷ with a call to our new function. We'll need a new search term, too. At ❸, we grab the first two letters of the last capitalized word. That should make for some interesting lowercase/uppercase and forward/backward searches.

Now that we have a few different tools for generating text, let's turn the randomness level up a notch.

7.3 A Test Monkey Could Do This Job

By this point, we've definitely made our test script a little more flexible. We use different input data each time through and a different way of driving each feature.

But we're still running the same general sequence of events: add text, hit Undo twice, check the answer, and so on. Let's try to be a bit more spontaneous. We're going to leave RSpec behind for a bit and enter the world of the *test monkey*, a script that bashes haphazardly at your program in order to help you shake out problems.

Of course, there's a catch. One advantage of using predictable inputs is that you know what the output should be. As you gradually introduce more randomness—I like to imagine a continuum like Figure 7.1—it becomes more difficult to define "passing" and "failing."

If all we're doing is clicking at random X/Y coordinates and typing meaningless keystrokes, it's nearly impossible to specify in advance what the application should do. The role of a test monkey is rather different from an RSpec script. Rather than a "spec that runs," it's more like a spotlight you can shine on an app to draw out the bugs.[3]

---

3. A test monkey that shines a light? Of *course* I'm calling this thing monkeyshines.rb!

Test monkeys come in many forms: some have no notion of UI elements and instead just treat the screen as a blank canvas for clicking, while others at least know how to press a button or select a menu item. For this chapter, we'll look at the latter.

We'll specifically exclude any actions that would exit the app. So if at any point LockNote isn't running, we may have crashed it. As you follow along with these tests, you may also find it interesting to keep an eye on the app and its memory consumption as it runs. You're in sleuth mode now, recording all these observations as clues.

Random (Inter)action

To pick a random GUI action to perform, we need a way to describe what actions are possible. That's exactly what def_action() from Section 7.1, *Action!*, on page 91 does. How convenient! All we have to do is dress it up with a little bookkeeping:

```ruby
require 'set'

class LockNote
  @@actions = Set.new

  def self.def_action(name, options)
    @@actions << name

    define_method name do
      # ...rest of method, as before
    end
  end
end
```

Each time we define a new GUI operation, LockNote will remember its name in @@actions. When it comes time to run our test monkey, we'll choose a bunch of random actions and turn 'em loose on the GUI. Set, by the way, is an often-overlooked utility class that comes with Ruby. It's like an Array with no duplicates.

We're not limited to just actions that can be expressed with def_action(). We can add any member function of LockNote to @@actions. For example, here are a couple of new ones for typing and clicking:

guessing/locknote.rb
```ruby
def random_typing
  num = 1 + rand(50)
  random_text = (1..num).collect {rand(26) + ?a}.pack 'c*'
  type_in random_text
  $logger.info "Typing #{random_text}"
end
```

```
def random_clicking
  num = 1 + rand(10)
  num.times do
    point = nil
    (rand(2) + 1).times do
      point = @main_window.click(EditControl, :left, point || :random)
      $logger.info "Clicking #{point.inspect}"
    end
  end
end
```

```
@@actions << :random_typing << :random_clicking
```

Now we can pound on LockNote by calling random_action() a bunch of times:

guessing/monkeyshines.rb

```
note = Note.open
100.times {note.random_action}
```

The test log will contain a full record of what we did. If we find a bug and want to try to re-create it, we can set the random seed and play the whole script back. But there's a way to get a little finer-grained control than that.

Data Can Be Code, Too

Right now, our log messages are plain English: "performing select_all from the menu bar" and so forth. Just as we transformed written examples into RSpec tests in previous chapters, let's turn our log files into Ruby programs. All it takes is a change of logging format. Here are replacements for all our calls to $logger.info():

```
# Menu bar
$logger.info "menu '#{action[0]}', '#{action[1]}'"

# Keyboard
$logger.info "keystroke " + action.join(', ') + "; sleep 0.5"

# Context menu
$logger.info "@main_window.click EditControl, :right; sleep 0.5"
$logger.info "type_in '#{action}'; sleep 0.5"

# Random typing
$logger.info "type_in '#{random_text}'"

# Random mousing
$logger.info "@main_window.click EditControl, :left, " + point.inspect
```

Now we can cut and paste sections of our test log into a Ruby script and replay just the parts we care about.

instance_eval() will let us run the code in the context of a single LockNote object:

guessing/replay.rb

```
require 'LockNote'

EditControl = LockNote::EditControl

Note.open.instance_eval do
  menu 'Edit', 'Select All'
  type_in 'asggzwhcbgk'
  keystroke 17, 90; sleep 0.5
  @main_window.click EditControl, :left, [370, 253]
  @main_window.click EditControl, :left, [370, 253]
  @main_window.click EditControl, :left, [644, 255]
  # ...
end
```

And there you have it. Our passive test log has become an active tool we can use to track down bugs. We've completed the cycle from code to data and back to code again.

7.4 Breaking Camp

What we've done in this chapter is dipped our toes into uncertainty. There are several ways we could make our test monkey more destructive (and therefore more effective):

- Get more sophisticated by adding dialog boxes (for passwords and searching) to our monkey's repertoire.
- Get more primitive by adding mouse dragging and a bigger palette of random characters to type.
- Rather than doing a fixed number of actions, keep pounding on LockNote until it exits and then report and start again.
- Answer questions more interesting than just "Is it running?" by using the Windows tasklist command to monitor memory usage and CPU time.

Those are all appealing variations on the theme. What I'd like to do now, though, is look at a completely different way to introduce diversity to a test project.

We have a good handle on changing one thing at a time—the characters our script is typing, for instance. In the next chapter, we're going break into two dimensions and try *combinations* of changes.

Whoa.

> ▶ Neo, and other Keanu characters

Chapter 8

Turn the Tables: Matrix Testing

In the previous chapter, we looked at several different ways to bring some variety into our tests. But we were typically changing just one thing at a time. There were three ways to paste text, so we had three different pasting tests.

What if we needed to run all three of those tests on, say, five different types of documents? We'd want to cover all fifteen combinations. That's the idea behind matrix testing.

In this chapter, we'll look at ways to express many different combinations of tests in a compact tabular format. In particular, we'll explore the two most popular Ruby libraries for matrix testing, ZenTest and RubyFIT.

But first, let's pick a different app to test. I'm ready for a break from the text editors we've been exercising.

8.1 What to Test

It'd be nice to test some kind of calculator. There are infinitely many combinations of numbers to test, which means we'll have to think carefully about boundary conditions and cases that are likely to fail.

Another SourceForge search reveals TimeCalc (see Figure 8.1, on the next page), an integer calculator that can add intervals of a day, hour, minute, or second.[1] Perfect! Not only will we be able to try different combinations of integers, but we can also test various unit conversions (from seconds to minutes, and so forth).

---

1. http://sf.net/projects/timecalc

Figure 8.1: TIMECALC

TimeCalc is an older app, so it needs one minor tweak to compile with recent Java versions. First, in your project folder, create a nested sub-sub-subdirectory called org/crocodile/timecalc and extract the source into it. Next, change line 284 of TimeCalc.java, where it says this...

```
helpd=new Dialog(null,"Help", true);
```

into this:

```
helpd=new Dialog((Frame)null,"Help", true);
```

Now the code will compile normally, with a few warnings we don't have to worry about for this chapter:

```
$ javac org/crocodile/timecalc/TimeCalc.java
Note: org/crocodile/timecalc/TimeCalc.java uses or overrides a deprecated API.
Note: Recompile with -Xlint:deprecation for details.
Note: org/crocodile/timecalc/TimeCalc.java uses unchecked or unsafe operations.
Note: Recompile with -Xlint:unchecked for details.
$ javac org/crocodile/timecalc/TimeCalcApp.java
Note: org/crocodile/timecalc/TimeCalcApp.java uses or overrides a deprecated API.
Note: Recompile with -Xlint:deprecation for details.
```

TimeCalc was written using the older AWT user interface library. Fortunately, JRuby and Jemmy can control AWT apps just fine; we just use names like Frame instead of JFrame:

```
require 'java'

$CLASSPATH << '.'
include_class 'org.crocodile.timecalc.TimeCalcApp'
include_class 'org.netbeans.jemmy.operators.FrameOperator'

TimeCalcApp.main(nil)
main_window = FrameOperator.new 'Time Calc'
```

I've written a simple Calculator class that drives the application using the same techniques we discussed in the first half of the book. Going into the details of the source code here would be repetitive. If you'd like to look at it on your own, you can find it in code/tables/calculator.rb.

8.2 ZenTest and the Art of Matrix Maintenance

ZenTest is an entire suite of testing tools from Ryan "zenspider" Davis and Eric Hodel that includes a matrix test library called FunctionalTest-Matrix. To use it, we just install ZenTest. . .

```
$ sudo jruby -S gem install ZenTest
```

and load the parts of ZenTest and Ruby's bundled Test::Unit that we need (plus RSpec, so our tests can still use the should notation inside):

tables/matrix.rb

```
require 'test/unit'
require 'test/unit/ui/console/testrunner'
require 'functional_test_matrix'
require 'spec'

Test::Unit::TestCase.extend FunctionalTestMatrix
```

Now we're ready to start writing tables.

Into the Matrix

We're going to look at one tiny slice of the calculator's functionality in this section. We'll add together a few different combinations of time spans and make sure that both addition and overflow detection work.

Let's think about some of the cases we want to test. The calculator doesn't allow negative numbers—but we should at least test with 0 and 1, a huge number near the upper end of the calculator's range, and also an uninteresting number like 2.[2] The table of expected behavior might look like this, then:

Addition	To 0...	To 1...	To 2...	To a Huge Number...
...add 0	0	1	2	Huge
...add 1	1	2	3	Huge + 1
...add 2	2	3	4	Overflow
...add a huge number	Huge	Huge + 1	Overflow	Overflow

---

2. Here come the angry letters from the Official Fan Club of 2!

We could test all sixteen combinations in RSpec, but it would be pretty verbose. Even if we pull out all the stops and use as many of RSpec's code-sharing features as we can, we can compress it only so far. Here's a single describe block from such an effort:

tables/calculator_spec.rb

```ruby
describe 'Starting with 1' do
  include AdditionHelper

  it_should_behave_like 'a new calculator'

  before do
    @calc.enter_number 1
    @calc.plus
  end

  it 'should add 0 correctly' do
    add_and_check(0, 1)
  end

  it 'should add 1 correctly' do
    add_and_check(1, 2)
  end

  # two more nearly-identical examples
end
```

By the time we fill in the other two examples, copy and paste the whole describe block four times, add the "new calculator" shared behavior, and implement AdditionHelper, we're well over 120 lines.

With ZenTest's FunctionalTestMatrix, we can write these different combinations much more compactly:

tables/matrix.rb

```ruby
class CalculatorTest
  matrix :addition, :to_0,   :to_1,    :to_2, :to_huge
  action :add_0,    0,       1,        2,     :huge
  action :add_1,    1,       2,        3,     :huge_1
  action :add_2,    2,       3,        4,     :over
  action :add_huge, :huge,   :huge_1,  :over, :over
end
```

Our matrix is done, but we still need to write support code to connect it to the calculator app.

Connecting the Matrix

The connecting code takes the form of CalculatorTest, a test case recognizable by Test::Unit:

`tables/matrix.rb`

```ruby
require 'calculator'

class CalculatorTest < Test::Unit::TestCase
  def setup
❶    @calc ||= Calculator.single
    @calc.clear
  end
end
```

At ❶, we're sharing a single instance of Calculator across all our tests, because the original calculator was written to exit the entire Java process when it's turned off. That would abort our test suite, so we should hit the Off button only at the very end of our script.

The idea behind FunctionalTestMatrix is that a matrix like this one. . .

```ruby
matrix :test_name,     :condition_a, :condition_b,
action :first_action,  :result_a1,   :result_b1,
action :second_action, :result_a2,   :action_a2,
```

will make the following sequence of calls to your test class:

```
setup
matrix_init_test_name(:condition_a)
matrix_setup_first_action(:condition_a, :result_a1)
matrix_test_result_a1(:condition_a)

setup
matrix_init_test_name(:condition_b)
matrix_setup_first_action(:condition_b, :result_b1)
matrix_test_result_b1(:condition_b)

setup
matrix_init_test_name(:condition_a)
matrix_setup_second_action(:condition_a, :result_a2)
matrix_test_result_a2(:condition_a)

setup
matrix_init_test_name(:condition_b)
matrix_setup_second_action(:condition_b, :result_b2)
matrix_test_result_b2(:condition_b)
```

So, you just define all those method names in your test class, and you are set. For the calculator, that means writing a lot of functions like matrix_setup_add1(), matrix_setup_add2(), matrix_test_3(), matrix_test_ overflow(), and so on. All those matrix_setup_add...() methods are going to look the same, except for the numbers they're adding. We'll just write a generic method_missing() that will transform matrix_setup_add1(:to_2, 3) into matrix_setup_add(1). Similarly, we'll turn matrix_test_3(:to_2) into matrix_test(3):

`tables/matrix.rb`

```ruby
class CalculatorTest
  alias_method :old_method_missing, :method_missing

  def method_missing(name, *args)
    case name.to_s
    when /matrix_setup_add_(.+)/
      matrix_setup_add $1
    when /matrix_test_(.+)/
      matrix_test $1
    else
      old_method_missing name, *args
    end
  end
end
```

All that's left is to write those test methods:

`tables/matrix.rb`

```ruby
class CalculatorTest
  Constants = {:huge => 2**63 - 2, :huge_1 => 2**63 - 1, :over => 0}

  def number_for(value)
    Constants[value.to_s.intern] || value.to_s.to_i
  end

  def matrix_init_addition(_, value)
    @seconds = number_for value
    @calc.enter_number @seconds
  end

  def matrix_setup_add(value)
    @adding = number_for value

    @calc.plus
    @calc.enter_number @adding
    @calc.equals
  end

  def matrix_test(expected)
    @calc.total_seconds.should == number_for(expected)
  end
end
```
❶

At ❶, we have a utility function that lets us treat actual numbers like 3 and names like :huge the same in our test cases.

After all the tests have run and Test::Unit has reported the results to us, we'll need to turn off the calculator. The simplest way to do this (though not the safest) is just to add a new TestCase class after CalculatorTest. The new pseudotest will delay for a bit to allow Test::Unit to finish its report and then shut down the calculator:

tables/matrix.rb
```
class CalculatorOff < Test::Unit::TestCase
  def test_off
    Thread.new {sleep 3; Calculator.single.off}
  end
end
```

Test::Unit runs test cases in the order it finds them in the file. So, CalculatorOff won't shut down the calculator until all the other steps have run.

Run matrix.rb. After the calculator gets put through its paces, you should see a report that sixteen test steps (plus our seventeenth "power-down" step) have passed.

Horror Vacui

Greek art from the Archaic period often packed every available space with details, in a style known as *horror vacui*, or "fear of empty space." It certainly seems we have a touch of horror vacui in our test matrix. Every possible combination of row and column has an expected result.

Testing all possible pairs of our selected numbers is probably a good idea for a calculator test. But for your own tests, you might have some combinations that aren't physically possible to get into from the user interface.

FunctionalTestMatrix allows you to put :na into any cell of the matrix to leave that row/column pair untested. If we were really sure that our calculator correctly treated addition as commutative (we shouldn't be so trusting!), we could remove about half the combinations like this, using the slightly more legible _ alias for :na.

```
tables/matrix.rb
```

```
class CalculatorTest
  _ = :na

  matrix :addition, :to_0,   :to_1,    :to_2, :to_huge
  action :add_0,     0,       _,        _,      _
  action :add_1,     1,       2,        _,      _
  action :add_2,     2,       3,        4,      _
  action :add_huge,  :huge,   :huge_1,  :over, :over
end
```

So, there you have it: a test table built in plain Ruby. What's next? How about finding a way to embed the results in the same table that describes the tests, instead of printing them at the end of our test run?

8.3 Fit to Be Tested

In 2002, Ward Cunningham created a testing library called the Framework for Integrated Test, or Fit. The idea was similar to our ZenTest example earlier: test authors could write their tests as tables, rather than as imperative programs.

But unlike ZenTest, where tables are written as Ruby code, Fit uses HTML as its test description language. So, any program that can save documents as web pages—a word processor, for instance—becomes a potential test-authoring tool. The goal was to make test writing easier for nonprogrammers. But a nice side effect of using HTML is that we can embed the results into the tables, right alongside the tests.

Getting Fit

Fit's original implementation language was Java, but it has been ported to many other languages, including (fortunately for us) Ruby:

```
$ sudo jruby -S gem install fit
```

A Fit "test script" is just an HTML file with a bunch of tables in it. Each table is considered an independent test fixture, whose behavior usually follows one of Fit's predefined fixture types.

Some fixtures are declarative in style: each row is a separate test case, and the order doesn't matter. Others are more like imperative programming languages: each row denotes one step of a process.

Column Fixtures

One of the key features of the time calculator is its ability to understand times that are entered in unusual ways. If you were to do some arithmetic with a time of 86,401 seconds, you'd probably expect the calculator to treat that value as if you had entered it the "official" way of one day, zero hours, zero minutes, and one second.

Here's a table that shows how the calculator should convert several combinations of hours, minutes, and seconds to more normal-looking formats (where the seconds and minutes range from 0 to 59 and the hours range from 0 to 23):

Days In	Hours In	Mins In	Secs In	Days Out	Hours Out	Mins Out	Secs Out
1	47	59	59	2	23	59	59
1	47	59	60	3	0	0	0
1	47	59	61	3	0	0	1
0	0	0	86399	0	23	59	59
0	0	0	86400	1	0	0	0
0	0	0	86401	1	0	0	1

This table translates almost directly into the HTML structure used by Fit's ColumnFixture class. The following code draws the table shown in Figure 8.2, on the following page:

`tables/TestTimeSample.html`

```
<table border="1">
  <tbody>
    <tr><td colspan="8">CalculateTime</td></tr>
    <tr>
      <td><em>days</em></td>
      <td><em>hours</em></td>
      <td><em>mins</em></td>
      <td><em>secs</em></td>

      <td><em>days()</em></td>
      <td><em>hours()</em></td>
      <td><em>mins()</em></td>
      <td><em>secs()</em></td>
    </tr>

    <tr>
      <td>1</td> <td>47</td> <td>59</td> <td>59</td>
      <td>2</td> <td>23</td> <td>59</td> <td>59</td>
    </tr>
    <tr>
      <td>1</td> <td>47</td> <td>59</td> <td>60</td>
      <td>3</td> <td>0</td>  <td>0</td>  <td>0</td>
    </tr>

    <!-- ... and so on -->
  </tbody>
</table>
```

CalculateTime							
days	*hours*	*mins*	*secs*	*days()*	*hours()*	*mins()*	*secs()*
1	47	59	59	2	23	59	59
1	47	59	60	3	0	0	0
1	47	59	61	3	0	0	1
0	0	0	86399	0	23	59	59
0	0	0	86400	1	0	0	0
0	0	0	86401	1	0	0	1
0	0	0	9223372036854775807	106751991167300	15	30	7

Figure 8.2: COLUMNFIXTURE, BEFORE TEST

All we had to do is change the column names to match Fit's conventions in the row beginning at ❶. For instance, instead of "days in" and "days out," we now have days and days(), respectively.

Fit will go through the table one row at a time, reading from left to right within each row. Inside each cell, it will look at the column name and either read or write an attribute of a test fixture object (we'll define that in a minute), depending on whether the column name ends in parentheses.

So, a value of 2 in the nonparenthesized days column would cause Fit to run something like the following pseudocode. . .

```
fixture.days = 2
```

whereas a 2 in the days() column (with parentheses) would read the attribute instead and check the result:

```
passed = (fixture.days == 2)
```

Where does Fit get that fixture object?[3] The title of the table is "Calculate-Time," so Fit will look in calculate_time.rb for a class called CalculateTime.

Let's put that class together. First, here's the initializer:

tables/calculate_time.rb

```
require 'fit/column_fixture'
require 'calculator'
```

---

3. Actually, Fit's internal name for this variable is adapter, but who's counting?

```
class CalculateTime < Fit::ColumnFixture
  def initialize
    @calc = Calculator.single
    @days = @hours = @mins = @secs = nil
  end
end
```

Next, we need to provide accessors for those attributes. Let's look at the pseudocode for how Fit will process a typical row of test data:

```
fixture.days  = 1
fixture.hours = 47
fixture.mins = 59
fixture.secs = 59

passed = (fixture.days == 2)
passed &&= (fixture.hours == 23)
passed &&= (fixture.mins == 59)
passed &&= (fixture.secs == 59)
```

❶

Not until ❶ do we have all four values that will be entered into the calculator. So, the only nontrivial accessor is the writer for secs. This one will do all the button pushing. It will enter the four numbers, add zero (which will cause the calculator to do the unit conversion), and parse the results:

tables/calculate_time.rb

```
class CalculateTime
  attr_accessor :days, :hours, :mins
  attr_reader :secs

  def secs=(value)
    @secs = value

    @calc.enter_time @days, @hours, @mins, @secs
    @calc.plus
    @calc.enter_number 0
    @calc.equals

    @days, @hours, @mins, @secs = @calc.time
  end
end
```

To run the test, we need a custom test harness to shut down the calculator at the end, just like we did with ZenTest. All we have to do is create our own copy of the fit file in <<fit directory>>/bin and add a custom test runner.

`tables/fit.rb`

```
class CalcRunner < Fit::FileRunner
  def run(args)
    process_args args
    process
    $stderr.puts @fixture.totals
    Calculator.single.off # will exit
  end
end

CalcRunner.new.run(ARGV)
```

Put that code in place of the line that calls Fit::FileRunner, and save it in your project directory as fit.rb. Now you can test the calculator like this:

```
$ jruby fit.rb TestTime.html TestTimeResults.html
```

Open TestTimeResults.html in your browser. You should see the same table that you started with, but with all the output columns (the ones with parentheses in the title) shaded light green to signify that the test passed, something like Figure 8.3, on the next page.

You'll notice that we've really tested only a few combinations of days, hours, minutes, and seconds—mostly near the edges of legal ranges. Go ahead and experiment with adding some more tests to the table. What kinds of values make good sense to try?

Action Fixtures

Of Fit's many different kinds of test fixtures, the column fixture we just discussed is the closest fit to this chapter's matrix-driven theme. But the action fixture is worth looking at as well.

An action fixture is more like a traditional test script: do this, press this, read this, check this value, and so on. Since we spent the first half of the book moving specific GUI actions *out* of the test script, I'm not going to take a whole lot of time putting them back in.

It's still worth writing a quick action fixture, just to get a feel for it. After all, if you have a project full of declarative Fit tests and you need to add only one or two sequential tests, creating a separate RSpec project for just those extra tests might be overkill.

CalculateTime							
days	hours	mins	secs	days()	hours()	mins()	secs()
1	47	59	59	2	23	59	59
1	47	59	60	3	0	0	0
1	47	59	61	3	0	0	1
0	0	0	86399	0	23	59	59
0	0	0	86400	1	0	0	0
0	0	0	86401	1	0	0	1
0	0	0	9223372036854775807	106751991167300	15	30	7

Figure 8.3: COLUMNFIXTURE, AFTER TEST

So, here's a simple addition test as an action fixture:

```
<table border="1">
  <tbody>
    <tr><td colspan="3">fit.ActionFixture</td></tr>
    <tr><td>start</td><td colspan="2">CalculatorActions</td></tr>
    <tr><td>enter</td><td>number</td><td>2</td></tr>
    <tr><td>press</td><td colspan="2">plus</td></tr>
    <tr><td>enter</td><td>number</td><td>3</td></tr>
    <tr><td>press</td><td colspan="2">equals</td></tr>
    <tr><td>check</td><td>total_seconds</td><td>5</td></tr>
  </tbody>
</table>
```

The first two rows of the table tell Fit to look for an ActionFixture called CalculatorActions in calculator_actions.rb. Each subsequent row contains one of three words Fit understands:

- enter x y passes whatever we supply for y to the x() method of our fixture.

- press x calls our fixture's x() method.

- check x y calls the x() method and compares the result with y.

As with the column fixture, Fit will color any pass/fail cells of the table according to their status.

We've now seen several different ways we can vary more than one parameter at once. Now we're left with the much more difficult task of choosing what conditions should vary and which combinations we should test.

Brian Marick's workshop materials provide a wonderful discussion on selecting effective test values.[4] It's also worth exploring the idea of *pairwise* testing, or covering many combinations with as few test cases as possible.[5]

What's next? Well, just as there are some tests that call out for a compact table representation, there are others that are best expressed in a lengthier narrative setting: a story.

So in a couple of chapters, we're going to test a simple web app with a set of readable, engaging stories. Ah, but first, how do we test web apps? Find out in the next chapter.

4. http://www.exampler.com/testing-com/writings/half-day-programmer.pdf
5. http://www.pairwise.org/articles.asp

The Internet is not something that you just dump something on. It's not a big truck. It's a series of tubes.
▶ Sen. Ted Stevens

## Chapter 9

Testing the Tubes: Web Applications

Ready to break out of the desktop for a little while? Let's test the GUIs of some web apps. There are several different tacks we could take.

- *Impersonating a browser*: A headless script sends the same kinds of requests a browser would but just measures response times without bothering to look at the content of the web page.

- *Parsing the HTML ourselves*: Start with the "impersonator," but add the ability to drill into the web page to identify links, buttons, text, and other GUI elements.

- *Driving an actual browser*: With this approach, a test script would launch, say, Firefox and cause it to fill in forms, visit links, etc.

So, are we impersonators, parsers, or drivers? All three, I hope.

The impersonator approach is good for finding bottlenecks in your app. You can quickly assemble a bunch of simple test nodes to hit your site at once and use something like Julian Boot's "Getting Real Numbers" technique to analyze the results.[1] When you need a little more sophistication, maybe for a quick-running functional test, you can parse the replies from the server with something like Webrat.[2]

But going through a real web browser is the closest to how your end users are going to see the app. And it's the only practical way to test

---

1. http://conferences.oreillynet.com/presentations/rails2007/boot_julian.pdf
2. http://agilewebdevelopment.com/plugins/webrat

JavaScript-heavy pages from a script. I hope you're using a mixture of all these techniques to test your web app. Since this is a GUI book, though, this chapter will focus on in-browser testing.

9.1 In-Browser Testing

In this chapter, we'll write a few simple scripts to exercise a single feature of a web application. The focus is on the nuts and bolts of controlling the browser, not on simulating a lengthy, interactive session on the site. For that, you'll have to wait until the next chapter.

Rather than directly parsing a web page's HTML, an in-browser test will launch a web browser and use some kind of scripting interface to direct the browser as it clicks buttons and follows links. The exact method of controlling the browser varies. Some browsers support their platforms' native automation interfaces, like Internet Explorer's COM bindings or Safari's AppleScript dictionary. The Watir family of test toolkits are simple wrappers around these specific APIs.

Other test libraries are more platform-independent. Selenium RC, for instance, acts as a local web proxy sitting between the real browser and the outside world. It injects its own JavaScript code into every page the browser sees, and test scripts interact with the provided JavaScript interface by sending Selenium simple commands over TCP.

No matter whether you're going through a simple Ruby/COM bridge or through three layers of JavaScript and network libraries, your top-level test script will have pretty much the same structure. In fact, for simple tests, it can consist of exactly the same code, as we'll see later.

9.2 Selenium

Selenium is a suite of web testing tools. It includes an IDE for writing scripts, an HTML-based scripting language called Selenese (a bit like Fit from the previous chapter), a TCP server for programming languages *other* than Selenese, and a few more goodies.

Covering all of Selenium would be a huge undertaking. We need only a couple of its technologies for this book: the Core engine that runs the tests inside a browser and the Remote Control server that lets us direct those tests from Ruby.

Hello, Selenium

The OpenQA folks offer an all-in-one Selenium package, with both the server software and the various programming language bindings (including Ruby).[3] However, I prefer to work "inside out." Rather than downloading a Selenium server that has its own Ruby files inside, I've installed a Ruby library that has its own copy of the Selenium server inside:

```
$ sudo gem install Selenium
```

It's important to capitalize Selenium's name just for the previous command; for the rest of this chapter, you'll spell it in all lowercase letters. The gem puts the selenium command in your PATH, so you can launch the server with one word. Go ahead and try it:

```
$ selenium
«bunch of startup messages»
20:47:41.895 INFO - Started SocketListener on 0.0.0.0:4444
```

Leave that running and grab another command line to run your tests.

A Taste of Web Testing

Let's see what it's like to drive a real web app. A search engine is a pretty intuitive concept, so we'll use the book search on the Pragmatic Programmers' website. We'll search for books on Ruby, parse through the detailed results, and select an item for the shopping cart.

We'll stop short of actually logging into the purchasing system. Andy and Dave were kind enough to let me use their site for this example, and I don't want to set loose tens of millions of readers[4] hammering on the accounts system for what's just supposed to be an example.[5]

Getting Connected

The first thing we need to do is load the main pragprog.com page. Take the Ruby code on the following page for a spin.

---

3. http://www.openqa.org/selenium-rc/download.action
4. I can dream, can't I?
5. Maybe those of you with last names from A–M can run the code examples on Monday/Wednesday/Friday, and N–Z can have Tuesday/Thursday. Weekends are for numbers and underscores.

```
tubes/selenium_example.rb
require 'rubygems'
require 'selenium'

browser = Selenium::SeleniumDriver.new \
❶   'localhost', 4444, '*firefox', 'http://www.pragprog.com', 10000

browser.start
browser.open 'http://www.pragprog.com'
```

At ❶, we connect to the Selenium server and tell it our browser preference. As you're running these tests, you might experiment by replacing *firefox with *iexplore, *safari, *opera, or one of the other Selenium-defined names.[6] When you run what you have so far. . .

```
$ ruby selenium_example.rb
```

you should end up with something like Figure 9.1, on the facing page. Selenium has inserted itself into the top half of the window; in the upper-right corner, you can see the list of actions it's performing.

Using a Search Form

Once we've started the browser and landed on a web page, how do we interact with it? For our simple search form smoke test, it'll probably suffice to type in a known search term and make sure a specific book pops up in the results.

So just for fun, let's search for book titles containing the word *Ruby*. Here's the core of the search form on the page we're going to use, simplified a bit:

```
<input id="q">
<button class="go">
```

And here's the Ruby code that will drive those controls using Selenium:

```
tubes/selenium_example.rb
❶   browser.type  '//input[@id="q"]', 'Ruby'
❷   browser.click '//button[@class="go"]'
    browser.wait_for_page_to_load 5000
```

Notice how the id=... and class=... identifiers at ❶ and ❷ parallel the form elements. These identifiers use XPath, a notation for describing the structure of XML documents (which also happens to work OK for HTML).[7]

---

6. Search http://wiki.openqa.org for *special browser strings*, or just visit http://tinyurl.com/2mp5dw.
7. http://www.w3.org/TR/xpath

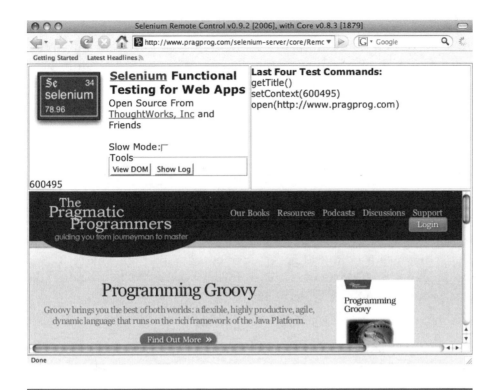

Figure 9.1: SELENIUM AND FIREFOX

XPath is a huge topic, and it's only one of several ways Selenium can use to find parts of a web page. So, in lieu of an all-encompassing tutorial, this chapter will just explain a few XPath concepts on the fly, as we encounter them.

Making Sense of the Results

The search form spits out a chunk of HTML that looks like this (minus the stuff we don't need for this example):

```
<table id="bookshelf">
  <tr>
    <td class="description">
      <h4><a href="http://pragprog.com/book-link">Book Title</a></h4>
      <p class="by-line">by One Author and Another Author, with One Helper</p>
    </td>
  </tr>
  ... rest of results ...
</table>
```

We have two tasks ahead of us: finding the number of search results (that is, rows in the table) and grubbing out a book's details (title, author, and so on) from each row. For the first task, Selenium provides a function, get_xpath_count(), once we conjure up the right XPath expression. Let's get conjurin'!

Counting the Rows

Here's how to look for <tr> elements inside the bookshelf table:

```
//table[@id="bookshelf"]/tr
```

However, some web browsers take it upon themselves to "clean up" the HTML and add extra tags while they're rendering a page. For example, sometimes a table will get a <tbody> tag added just inside it. So, the previous XPath expression won't always work. We can modify the expression to watch for <tbody>, like this:

```
//table[@id="bookshelf"]/tbody/tr
```

But that will fail on browsers that *don't* modify the HTML. For this example, we'll just go with an expression that will match both:

```
//table[@id="bookshelf"]//tr
```

This will match any <tr> inside the table, even if it's buried inside a sub-subtable. Fortunately, this page doesn't use nested tables.

Now that we have an XPath expression that will match any row inside the table, Selenium's get_xpath_count() function will tell us the number of rows in the table:

tubes/selenium_example.rb

```
num_results = browser.get_xpath_count('//table[@id="bookshelf"]//tr').to_i
```

Not all projects hand us such a simple layout on a silver platter. Sometimes, you end up with really hard-to-write, fragile XPath expressions with lots of nested div/div/div/p/span/a stuff. Fortunately, there are ways to cut across all those layers. Let's look at one of those ways as we iterate through the search results.

Looping Through the Results

Each search result is an <a> within an <h4> within a <td> within a <tr> within a <table>. So to find, say, the third result, we could use this:

```
//table[@id="bookshelf"]/tr[3]/td/h4/a
```

Aside from the earlier <tbody> issue, this expression specifies five layers of HTML structure directly. That can be kind of fragile in the face of change. Instead, let's jump right into the table and look for <td class="description"> tags. A first attempt might look like this:

```
//td[@class="description"][3]/h4/a
```

But that would match only the third <td class="description"> in a table row. This table doesn't have any three-element rows. What we want is the third <td class="description"> anywhere on the page. The descendant modifier (XPath calls it the descendant "axis") allows us to write a little more general version:

```
descendant::td[@class="description"][3]/h4/a
```

Here's how to put it all together:

tubes/selenium_example.rb
```
results = (1..num_results).map do |n|
❶   element = "xpath=/descendant::td[@class='description'][#{n}]/h4/a"
    title   = browser.get_text(element)
❷   url     = browser.get_attribute(element + '@href')

    {:title => title, :url => url, :element => element}
end

results.each do |r|
  puts 'Title: ' + r[:title]
  puts 'Link:  ' + r[:url]
  puts
end
```

The expression at ❶ finds the nth <td class="description"> item anywhere on the page and then drills into it to get the hyperlink. The leading xpath= isn't part of the XPath standard. It's an extra hint for Selenium, which needs to be explicitly told we're using XPath if our expression starts with anything other than //.

Using descendant is overkill for this fairly simple layout. But when you have a big, complicated page to parse and no easy id or class attributes to grab hold of, the fancier XPath axes may be the only way to specify what you're looking for. Just be aware that the more general the expression, the more you risk matching more items on the page than you intended.

Jumping Off the Site

So far, all the links we've followed and forms we've filled out have stayed within the same domain. If you happen to need to follow a link to another site, you'll need to be aware of one of Selenium's subtleties.

Let's continue from the previous example, where we looked through a list of search results. If we now click a book's title...

`tubes/selenium_example.rb`
```
pickaxe = results.find {|r| r[:title].include? 'Programming Ruby 3'}
browser.click pickaxe[:element]
browser.wait_for_page_to_load 5000
```

we'll get a full details page, including a "Buy Now" form that looks a little like this:

```
<form id="buy-now">
  <div>
    <label>Select a Format:</label>
    <select name="sku_id">
      ... book format options ...
    </select>
    <button class="add-to-cart" type="submit">
      <span>Add to Cart</span>
    </button>
  </div>
</form>
```

Let's add some code to put the book in our cart and then log in to make the purchase. Note the secure URL of the login link: we're moving from http:// to https://.

`tubes/selenium_example.rb`
```
browser.click '//button[@class="add-to-cart"]'
browser.wait_for_page_to_load 5000

browser.open 'https://secure.pragprog.com/login'
browser.wait_for_page_to_load 5000
```

What happens when you run the code now? Probably something like this:

```
«path»/selenium.rb:162:in `do_command': Permission denied to get property
Location.href (SeleniumCommandError)
```

Here's why we're seeing an error. Remember that the Selenium server injects its JavaScript libraries on the fly into each page we visit. Since we're testing pages that live at pragprog.com, the web browser has been fooled into thinking that the http://pragprog.com domain is hosting all that JavaScript. Because of the "same-origin" security policy, your browser won't let those scripts control pages on any other domain.[8] And the secure https://pragprog.com domain is considered different from the regular http://pragprog.com domain.

Fortunately, there's a workaround. In addition to all the supported browsers we discussed earlier (*iexplore, *firefox, and so on), Selenium allows a couple of experimental browser strings, *iehta and *chrome.

These control Internet Explorer and Firefox, respectively, but using their native scripting interfaces rather than vanilla JavaScript injected into a page.

These will do the trick, but be aware that you're bypassing an important safeguard. Ideally, you should be in control of the content of whatever page you're going to land on.

Go ahead and adjust the connection line of your test script to use one of the experimental browsers:

```
browser = Selenium::SeleniumDriver.new \
  'localhost', 4444, '*chrome', 'http://www.pragprog.com', 10000
```

The example should successfully land on the login page now.

9.3 Selenium and RSpec

Just as we did with the desktop apps we tested in the first half of this book, we're going to take a batch of the interface-specific code we have so far and package it up in a nice RSpec test. It's good practice, and it'll come in handy later in the chapter.

Searching with Class

The first thing we'll do is put all that browser-specific stuff inside a BookSearch class, as shown on the following page.

---

8. http://www.mozilla.org/projects/security/components/same-origin.html

`tubes/book_selenium.rb`

```ruby
require 'rubygems'
require 'selenium'

class BookSearch
  def initialize
    @browser = Selenium::SeleniumDriver.new \
      'localhost', 4444, '*firefox', 'http://www.pragprog.com', 10000
    @browser.start
  end

  def close
    @browser.stop
  end
end
```

Now, let's give the class a find() method that returns a title-indexed list of all books matching any given search term:

`tubes/book_selenium.rb`

```ruby
class BookSearch
❶ ResultCounter = '//table[@id="bookshelf"]//tr'
  ResultReader = 'xpath=/descendant::td[@class="description"]'

  def find(term)
    @browser.open '/'
    @browser.type  '//input[@id="q"]', term
    @browser.click '//button[@class="go"]'
    @browser.wait_for_page_to_load 5000

    num_results = @browser.get_xpath_count(ResultCounter).to_i

    (1..num_results).inject({}) do |results, i|
❷     full_title = @browser.get_text("#{ResultReader}[#{i}]/h4/a")
      byline = @browser.get_text("#{ResultReader}[#{i}]/p[@class='by-line']")
      url = @browser.get_attribute("#{ResultReader}[#{i}]/h4/a@href")

      title, subtitle = full_title.split ': '
❸     authors = authors_from byline

      results.merge title =>
      {
        :title => title,
        :subtitle => subtitle,
        :url => url,
        :authors => authors
      }
    end
  end
end
```

The XPath expressions at ❶ are the same as earlier in the chapter. We're just stashing them in constants to keep their purpose clear so we don't have to repeat ourselves so much at ❷.

Pulling author and contributor names from the byline at ❸ requires a bit of regular expressing matching:

`tubes/book_selenium.rb`

```ruby
class BookSearch
  def authors_from(byline)
    byline[3..-1].gsub(/(,? and )|(,? with )/, ',').split(',')
  end
end
```

Now we have a BookSearch class that could easily be modified to support any book search engine we care to (or any web browser we care to, as we'll soon see).

A Few Examples

Let's see what it would look like to call this code from some RSpec tests:

`tubes/search_spec.rb`

```ruby
describe 'Searching for Ruby' do
  before :all do
    @search = BookSearch.new
    @results = @search.find 'Ruby'
  end

  after :all do
    @search.close
  end

  it 'should find the Pickaxe book' do
    book = @results['Programming Ruby']
    book.should_not be_nil
    book[:authors].should include('Dave Thomas')
  end

  it 'should not find the Ajax book' do
    @results.should_not have_key('Pragmatic Ajax')
  end

  it 'should fail (on purpose) to find Gilgamesh' do
❶    @results.should have_key('Gilgamesh')
  end
end
```

I've added an intentional failure at ❶ so that we can look at ways to report problems. For reasons that will become clear later, I haven't put a require line in the spec file. So, you'll need to specify the book_selenium library on the command line.

```
$ spec -rbook_selenium search_spec.rb
```

Give that a shot. The text report will mention the one failed test, but what if we'd like to do something a little more informative?

Fancy Reporting

RSpec includes a lovely HTML formatter:

```
$ spec -fhtml -rbook_selenium search_spec.rb
```

That will print nice syntax-colored source code of whatever failures it encounters. And with just a small twist, we can add screenshots, too. Add a new Ruby file called html_capture.rb. First we'll use RSpec's config hooks to take a screenshot after every test step:

tubes/html_capture.rb

```
require 'spec/runner/formatter/html_formatter'

Spec::Runner.configure do |config|
  config.before :all do
    $example_num = 1
  end

  config.after do
❶   `screencapture #{$example_num}.png`
    $example_num += 1
  end
end
```

Using global variables is about the crudest way to keep track of which step we're on, but it'll do for a simple example like this. The screencapture call at ❶ is Mac-specific. If you're on Windows, you'll need to install the RMagick and win32capture gems and then replace that code with something like this:

```
width, height, bmp = Win32::Screenshot.foreground
Magick::Image.from_blob(bmp)[0].write "#{$example_num}.png"
```

Now RSpec will take a screen capture after every example. To include just the failed ones in our report, we'll create a new report formatter:

tubes/html_capture.rb

```
class HtmlCapture < Spec::Runner::Formatter::HtmlFormatter
  def extra_failure_content(failure)
    img = %Q(<img src="#{example_number}.png"
                alt="" width="25%" height="25%" />)
    super(failure) + img
  end
end
```

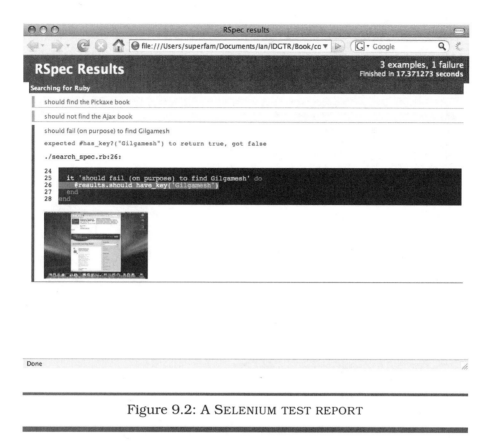

Figure 9.2: A SELENIUM TEST REPORT

To use our custom formatter, we use the command line both to load the new Ruby file and to specify the formatter class:

```
$ spec -rhtml_capture -fHtmlCapture -rbook_selenium search_spec.rb > out.html
```

After the test runs, open out.html in your browser. You should see something like Figure 9.2.

There are lots of potential improvements to this approach. We're not really using the screenshots of the passed steps, so perhaps we can skip taking them. We could turn the <img> tag into a link. We could detect which OS we're running and automatically use the appropriate screen capture method.

There is a Ruby gem called Spec::Ui that does all this. As of this writing, it's a couple of versions behind RSpec, but it's still worth looking into.[9]

---

9. http://rspec-ext.rubyforge.org

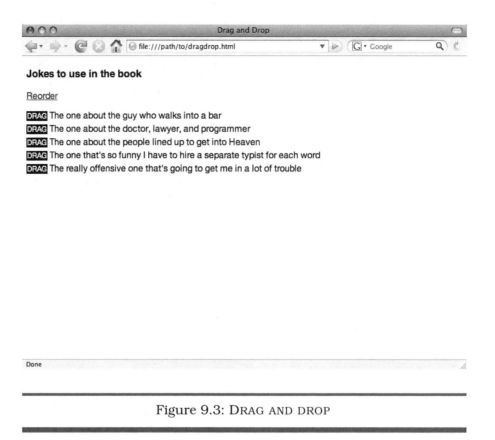

Figure 9.3: Drag and drop

We've seen an overview of how RSpec and Selenium plug into each other. Now, let's look at one place where Selenium outshines other web-testing toolkits: mouse-driven Ajax sites.

9.4 Interacting with Ajax

So far, we've looked only at straight HTML pages. How do we test something a little more interactive, like a JavaScript-heavy site?

For this section, we'll use a simple drag-and-drop list. I've included one in the source code for this book, in dragdrop.html. To use it, you'll need an open source JavaScript library called script.aculo.us.[10]

---

10. http://script.aculo.us

Download and open the latest source archive from script.aculo.us site. Copy all the .js files from the lib and src directories to the same folder where you're keeping dragdrop.html.

Open dragdrop.html manually in your browser, and click the "Reorder" link. If the JavaScript files are in the right place, then you should see a bunch of little black draggable handles, as in Figure 9.3, on the facing page.

Selenium works best when the browser is going through an actual web server, rather than just reading files off a disk. For the tests in this section, fire up a separate command prompt, and run the trivial Ruby-based server included in this chapter's source code (web_server.rb).[11] I'm assuming you're running behind a firewall or taking some other measure to keep people from hitting this page from the outside world.

Let's write a couple of tests to exercise the drag-and-drop capabilities of the joke list. First, here's the outline of the RSpec description:

```
require 'joke_list'

describe JokeList do
  before do
    @list = JokeList.new
  end

  after do
    @list.close
  end

  # tests will go here...
end
```

For the first example, we'll just do a single drag to the end of the list:

tubes/list_spec.rb
```
it 'lets me drag an item to the end' do
  @list.order('doctor').should == 2
  @list.move 2, 5
  @list.order('doctor').should == 5
end
```

Let's go ahead and fill in enough of the JokeList class to drive the web browser for that example.

---

11. Or you can use your favorite web server package and adjust the port numbers in the script if you want to use something other than 8000.

Here's the setup and teardown code:

`tubes/joke_list.rb`

```ruby
require 'rubygems'
require 'selenium'

class JokeList
  def initialize
    @browser = Selenium::SeleniumDriver.new \
      'localhost', 4444, '*firefox', "http://localhost:8000", 10000

    @browser.start
    @browser.open 'http://localhost:8000/dragdrop.html'
  end

  def close
    @browser.stop
  end
end
```

JokeList also needs an order() method so we can see where a given joke is in the list. I've given each joke a unique id attribute in the HTML, and Selenium's get_element_index() method will take those IDs directly:

`tubes/joke_list.rb`

```ruby
class JokeList
  def order(item)
    @browser.get_element_index(item).to_i + 1
  end
end
```

Now we need to add drag and drop. There are a few different ways to do this in Selenium. If we're just doing something really simple like moving an item past the end of a list, we can say this. . .

```ruby
@browser.drag_and_drop element, '0, +300'
```

which will break as soon as we try to test a list that's taller than 300 pixels. Coordinates retrieved at runtime are much more resilient than hard-coded offsets:

```ruby
last_y = @browser.get_element_position_top(last_element) +
         @browser.get_element_height(last_element)
@browser.drag_and_drop element, "0, #{last_y}"
```

But it turns out Selenium lets us specify the drop target directly:

```ruby
@browser.drag_and_drop_to_object element, last_element
```

Here's what it looks like in context:

`tubes/joke_list.rb`

```ruby
class JokeList
  Reorder = '//a[@id="reorder"]'
❶ Draggable = 'selenium.browserbot.findElement("css=.drag").visible()'
  Locked = '!' + Draggable

  def move(from_order, to_order)
    from_element = "//li[#{from_order}]/span[@class='drag']"
    to_element   = "//li[#{to_order}]/span[@class='drag']"

    @browser.click Reorder
❷   @browser.wait_for_condition Draggable, 2000

    @browser.drag_and_drop_to_object from_element, to_element

    @browser.click Reorder
❸   @browser.wait_for_condition Locked, 2000
  end
end
```

One thing to note is that XPath uses 1 to denote the first item in a list, rather than the 0 we're used to from Ruby. To keep things straight, I'm using order or pos for XPath-style, 1-based positions, and index for Ruby-style, 0-based indices.

Another thing we need to worry about is timing. When you're testing an Ajax page, you often need to wait for a portion of a page to refresh. To simulate a server round-trip, dragdrop.html pauses slightly before showing the drag handles when you click the "Reorder" link.

A naïve approach would be to add a fixed delay to our test script. But those are awfully prone to breakage. Instead, we're using Selenium's handy wait_for_condition() method at ❷ and ❸. This function will wait until a given JavaScript piece evaluates to true. To access elements on the page Selenium is controlling, you go through the browserbot attribute, like we're doing at ❶.

We'll write one more example—something a little more substantial—and move on. Just for fun, let's implement an alphabetic sort on the list. An end user might do something like an insertion sort: visually scan the list for the item that should go last, move it to the end, scan for the item that should be next-to-last, and so forth.[12]

---

12. Yes, it's $O(n^2)$ comparisons, but that's how people work.

`tubes/list_spec.rb`

```
it 'lets me drag multiple items to sort' do
  original = @list.items

  original.length.downto(1) do |last_pos|
    subset = @list.items[0..last_pos - 1]
    max_pos = subset.index(subset.max) + 1
    @list.move max_pos, last_pos
  end

  @list.items.should == original.sort
end
```

This new example requires us to be able to retrieve the current order of the jokes:

`tubes/joke_list.rb`

```
class JokeList
  def items
    num_items = @browser.get_xpath_count('//li').to_i
    (1..num_items).map {|i| @browser.get_text "//li[#{i}]/span[2]"}
  end
end
```

There's a lot more to interactive web pages than just drag and drop, of course. But we've touched on several places where Selenium does fairly well, including mouse input and waiting for state changes, both cornerstones of rich Internet apps.

9.5 Watir

Selenium is the big kid on the block of web application testing. It's open source, cross-platform, and based on readily available technology, and it works with almost any programming language. Sometimes that's overkill for what you need. Sometimes you want something that's not language-neutral but that's designed expressly for Ruby.

Designed for Ruby

That's the thinking behind Watir (Web Application Testing in Ruby).[13] Rather than trying to be all things to all people, it aims to provide a familiar experience specifically for Ruby developers.

---

13. http://wtr.rubyforge.org

In Selenium, you have one big, monolithic browser object that supports the typical operations: clicking, typing, dragging, and so on. By contrast, Watir uses a separate, small Ruby object for each little chunk of HTML that you specify.

So instead of this...

```
browser.get_text('//div[@id="foo"]/p')
```

you get the following:

```
browser.div(:id, 'foo').p.text
```

It's much easier and more natural from a Ruby standpoint to specify objects in Watir.

Of course, there's a trade-off. The original Watir supports only Internet Explorer. There is a separate library called SafariWatir, which, as the name implies, drives the Safari browser on the Mac. But it's a newer project, and many of Watir's features (such as searching for an element by class or XPath) are not yet implemented.

There's also FireWatir for Firefox on Windows, Mac, or Linux. It relies on a binary Firefox extension called JSSh that, as of this writing, presents a few installation challenges.

Using Watir with RSpec

It's relatively easy to convert the book search example from the first half of this chapter to Watir. Of course, the top-level test code doesn't need to change at all. Only the BookSearch class will need to be adapted. Here's the setup and teardown code:

tubes/book_watir.rb

```ruby
require 'rubygems'
require 'watir'

class BookSearch
  def initialize
    @browser = Watir::IE.new
  end

  def close
    @browser.close
  end
end
```

No big surprises there. Here's the new implementation of find():

```
tubes/book_watir.rb
class BookSearch
  def find(term)
    @browser.goto 'http://www.pragprog.com'
❶   @browser.text_field(:id, 'q').set('Ruby')
❷   @browser.button(:class, 'go').click

    bookshelf = @browser.table(:id, 'bookshelf')
    num_results = bookshelf.row_count

    (1..num_results).inject({}) do |results, i|
❸     book = bookshelf[i][2]

      full_title = book.h4(:index, 1).text
      byline     = book.p(:class, 'by-line').text
      url        = book.link(:index, 1).href

      title, subtitle = full_title.split ': '
      authors = authors_from byline

      results.merge title => {
        :title => title,
        :subtitle => subtitle,
        :url => url,
        :authors => authors }
    end
  end
end
```

The first thing you noticed was probably the way Watir accesses the form elements at ❶ and ❷. The text_field() and button() methods return individual Ruby wrappers around those controls.

It's not just form controls that get this treatment. Watir also provides the most common HTML tags, like the h4() and p() methods we call to retrieve the results.

Tables also act like fairly well-behaved Ruby objects in that they can be indexed with [], as at ❸, or iterated over using each, and so on. (They're not full-fledged Ruby Enumerables, though.)

To run the test, we just pass in the path to the new implementation of BookSearch on the command line:

```
$ spec -rbook_watir search_spec.rb
```

You should see the same results that you did with Selenium.

9.6 Wrapping Up

We've hit the highlights of controlling a browser from a script and driving a web page. The scripts we've seen have all been at a pretty superficial level of detail, though. They were enough to get us up and running in Selenium and Watir. But it would be nice to see a little more realistic of an example.

To do that, we're going to need some more of RSpec's expressiveness. Read on to find out how to craft richer tests that can simulate a lengthy user interaction with an app.

Chapter 10

Testing in Plain English: Story Runner

We've seen tests that look like cocktail napkins, and we've seen more compact tests that look like tables. They can be sort of legible to non-technical readers, but it still takes someone who knows Ruby to actually write them—to know where to put all those parentheses and do/end blocks and so forth.

What if the top-level tests could do away with Ruby syntax altogether and just be in plain text? That's the premise of Story Runner, a recent addition to RSpec.

10.1 From Examples to Stories

RSpec really has two sides to it. The "classic" describe/it notation, also known as *example* notation, is typically used for code-level unit tests. As you saw in the first half of the book, it also came in handy for library-level functional testing of the LockNote and JunqueNote classes we wrote.

The newer Story Runner is more geared toward user acceptance tests. The emphasis is on legibility over conciseness. At the time of this writing, Story Runner is still a relatively recent addition to RSpec. But it's rapidly becoming the preferred way of writing user interface tests.

Review: What Are Examples For?

Consider the following test that we saw earlier in Chapter 5, *The Home Stretch*, on page 61:

```
describe 'A previously saved document' do
  it_should_behave_like 'a saved document'
  it_should_behave_like 'a reopened document'

  it 'supports changing the password' do
    @note.change_password \
      :old_password => 'password',
      :password => 'new'
    @note.exit!

    @note = Note.open 'SavedNote', :password => 'new'
    @note.should_not have_prompted(:with_error)
    @note.should be_running
  end
end
```

This code exercised the change_password() method of the Note class. Since it was testing just one feature under one set of circumstances, it used a prefab test fixture instead of creating a new document from scratch.

The describe/it example has given us some degree of confidence that change_password() pushes the right GUI buttons to set a document's password. Now it's time to actually *use* that function in some acceptance tests.

Starting with Stories

Let's look at how we might use Story Runner to write a user acceptance test. Rather than exercise the app feature by feature, the way we did when we were doing functional testing, we're going to look at broader descriptions that might cover several features—user stories, in other words.[1]

For LockNote and JunqueNote, we might imagine a couple of general things people expect out of the app: password protection of documents and basic text-editing features. In Story Runner parlance, each of these would be considered a *story*.

---

1.   If you're a fan of agile software development, you've probably encountered the idea of user stories in a similar, but not identical, context. Dan North explains RSpec's specific take on stories at http://dannorth.net/whats-in-a-story.

Within, say, the password story, there are several different ways an end user could interact with the program. He might create a new document, save it, rename it, reopen it, get the password wrong on the first try, and finally view the contents. Or he might open an existing document, add some text at the end, and then change the password. Each of these scripted interactions is called a *scenario* in RSpec.

In RSpec, a story starts with a name and a free-form description. The latter can be anything; the custom is to follow the basic pattern, "As a *«role»*, I want to *«do something»* so that I can *«get some result»*."

Let's see how that concept looks for our password-changing example:

`story/password.story`

```
Story: Password protection

As a security-conscious person
I want to encrypt each document with a password
So that only I (and the NSA) can read it
```

Good. Now for the individual test steps.

Scenarios in a Story

There are lots of facets to passwords: how to create one, when to enter one, how to change one, what to do with a bad one, and so on. If we were creating a new app from scratch, we'd sketch out several different scenarios of the different ways people might lock and unlock documents. They'd all go under the general umbrella of the password protection story.

Imagine one of these specific scenarios of how someone might use a note-taking app in the real world:

1. Open a new document.
2. Type some text.
3. Save the document with a password.
4. Exit the program.
5. Use the old password to reopen the document.
6. Change the password from the old one to the new one.
7. Exit the program.
8. Use the new password to reopen the document.

Much as a describe block groups individual examples together, a Story contains one or more Scenarios. Each of these Scenarios follows a consistent script: "Given *«some condition»*, When *«I perform some action»*, Then

«I expect a particular result»." The previous list is pretty easy to rewrite in this format:

`story/password.story`

```
Scenario: Changing the password
  Given a new document
  When I type "this is my document"
  And I save the document as "Secrets" with password "unguessable"
  And I exit the app
  And I open the document "Secrets" with password "unguessable"
  Then the app should be running
  And the text should be "this is my document"

  When I change the password from "unguessable" to "uncrackable"
  And I exit the app
  And I open the document "Secrets" with password "uncrackable"
  Then the app should be running
  And the text should be "this is my document"
```

The idea is that someone close to the customer will write these stories and that someone familiar with Ruby (possibly the same person, but not necessarily) will write the test code that implements them.

Pattern Matching in Scenarios

So, how *do* we link these textual stories to all those Ruby calls that type keystrokes? RSpec uses a simple pattern-matching method. For each Given, When, or Then line in the plain-text user story, we need to write a corresponding chunk of Ruby code to implement that test step. RSpec sensibly calls these *step definitions*. Here's what a step definition file looks like:

`story/password.rb`

```
require 'rubygems'
require 'spec/story'

❶ steps_for :app_state do
  Given 'a new document' do
    @note = Note.open
  end

  When 'I exit the app' do
    @note.exit!
  end

  Then 'the app should be running' do
    @note.should be_running
  end
end
```

The steps_for line at ❶ groups a series of related definitions. Each Given, When, or Then block will run when RSpec encounters a matching phrase inside a scenario.

The matching algorithm has a little flexibility to it. A step introduced with And will be read as if it began with whatever the previous starting word was. So, the stilted When X / When Y / When Z becomes the more fluid When X / And Y / And Z.

Step definitions can be plain strings or regular expressions. They can have parameters, too:

`story/password.rb`

```
steps_for :documents do
  When 'I type "$something"' do |something|
    @note.text = something
  end

❶ When 'I save the document as "$name" with password "$password"' do
    |name, password|
    @note.save_as name, :password => password
  end

  When 'I open the document "$name" with password "$password"' do
    |name, password|
    @note = Note.open name, :password => password
  end

  When 'I change the password from "$old" to "$password"' do
    |old, password|
    @note.change_password :old_password => old, :password => password
  end

  Then 'the text should be "$something"' do |something|
    @note.text.should == something
  end
end
```

At ❶, you can see how step parameters are assigned. Each dollar variable inside the string is a placeholder for one parameter, and they're passed into the block in left-to-right order. The names of the dollar variables don't have to match the block parameters—I could have called them $1 and $2—but it's nice to be consistent.

RSpec will look for matches in the same order that you give the step definitions. So, When I eat will match When "I $verb" if it appears before When "I eat", even though the latter is more specific.

You've no doubt noticed that we haven't yet connected the step definitions in password.rb with the user story in password.story. Here's how to
do that. Notice that step groups are *composable*—we can specify that
RSpec should use both the app_state and documents groups for pattern
matching as it runs the tests:

story/password.rb

```
with_steps_for :app_state, :documents do
  run 'password.story'
end
```

Go ahead and give it a shot:

```
C:\> ruby -rlocknote password.rb
```

Here's the JRuby equivalent:

```
$ jruby -rjunquenote password.rb
```

So, what have we done? We've written a test in about three times the
number of lines it would have taken us in "classic" RSpec. After all the
emphasis on efficient notation, why would we want to write something
so wordy?

User stories are quite a bit wordier than their cocktail-napkin counter-
parts, but this verbosity can be useful. For instance:

- Writing stories in plain text helps close the loop from customer
  wishes to running code.
- When you find a bug in software, capturing it in a story can help
  the developers re-create the problem.
- In contrast to the petite examples that exercise a single feature,
  a story is a good fit for a long test that simulates a complex user
  interaction and may touch on many features.

10.2 Designing with Stories

Most of the sample apps we've tested in this book have been real-world
programs that existed long before the book did. That gave us the chance
to see the typical gotchas and caveats that would be missing from a toy
demo program.

But if we used someone else's preexisting app for this chapter, we'd
miss out on one place where stories really come in handy: documenting
designs *before* you have a real app. To get a feel for this process, we'll
build a web program from the ground up.

No-Hassle Party Invitations

What kind of site should we build? Here's an idea I wish someone would implement. We're all tired of those party-planning sites that send guests a 100KB GIF-laden email invitation that doesn't actually tell them anything about the party. Or that make you go through a million "easy steps" just to ask a few friends over for dinner.

Let's go to the other extreme and imagine a site where all the details are right there on the page and no registrations or email addresses are required at all. Ideally, all we should have to do is name the party; even the time should be a reasonable default. We'll call our site "Novite," as in "no-hassle invite."

Getting Started

The source code to Novite comes with this book. It just happens to be written in Ruby (using the Rails framework), but it could have been written in anything. The tests we're writing here aren't going to interact with the app's Ruby source at all; everything is going to go through the browser.

To drive the web browser, we're going to use Selenium RC. As we did in the previous chapter, we'll launch the Selenium server and leave it running during our tests. Our test code will use the Ruby wrapper for Selenium to send commands to the server.

So, you'll have two servers running during the test: the web server and Selenium RC. First, if you don't already have Rails installed, you'll need to do so:

```
$ sudo gem install -y rails
```

Then, go to where you put the source for this book and hop into the novite subdirectory. Before the first time you launch the app, you'll need to create the database:

```
$ rake db:migrate
```

Now you're ready to start the web server:

```
$ ruby script/server
```

Leave that running in its own terminal, start the Selenium server in a second terminal like we did in the previous chapter, and do your testing from a third one:

```
$ selenium
```

Ready to write the first story?

Sending Invitations

The first thing that happens is that the host has to plan the party. And we want that to happen with no preliminary steps: no registration, no giving out of email addresses, just party planning:

story/invite.story

```
Story: minimalist invites
  As a host with lots to do
  I want to plan a party with a minimum of mouse clicks
  So that I can get on with the rest of my tasks

  Scenario: manual invites
    Given a party called "Celebration"
    And a description of "There's a party goin' on"
    And a location of "Right here"
    And a starting time of September 29, 2010 at 12:30 PM
    And an ending time of September 29, 2010 at 12:35 PM

    When I view the invitation
    Then I should see the Web address to send to my friends
    And the name should be "Celebration"
    And the description should be "There's a party goin' on"
    And the location should be "Right here"
    And the party should begin on September 29, 2010 at 12:30 PM
    And the party should end on September 29, 2010 at 12:35 PM
```

Although this isn't Ruby, Ruby can be taught to understand it. Let's do that now. We could put Selenium calls directly in the step definitions, like this:

```
steps_for :invite do
  Given 'a party called "$name"' do |name|
    @browser = Selenium::SeleniumDriver.new \
      'localhost', 4444, '*firefox', 'http://localhost:3000', 10000
    @browser.start
    @browser.open '/parties/new'
    @browser.type 'id=party_name', name
  end
end
```

But that becomes unwieldy quickly, even for this trivial app. So, all the specific stuff about browsers and forms and links is going to go into a Party class, which we'll define in party.rb in a moment. First, though, let's take care of that middle layer—the step definitions.

Rather than starting and stopping our browser for each individual scenario, it'd be nice to create one Selenium object that will stick around for the entire test. RSpec makes this task pretty easy.

The Story Runner offers a steady stream of feedback on its progress by sending messages to a "listener" object you supply: story_started(), scenario_succeeded(), and so on. We can keep the web browser around for as long as we need it by listening for the run_started() and run_ended() callbacks:

`story/novite_stories.rb`

```ruby
require 'rubygems'
require 'spec/story'
require 'chronic'
require 'party'

class Listener
  attr_reader :browser

  def run_started(num_scenarios)
    @browser = Selenium::SeleniumDriver.new \
      'localhost', 4444, '*firefox', 'http://localhost:3000', 10000
    @browser.start
  end

  def run_ended
    @browser.stop
  end

  def method_missing(name, *args, &block)
    # We don't care about the rest of the Story Runner events.
  end
end

listener = Listener.new
Spec::Story::Runner.register_listener(listener)
```

We'll be ready to define the first batch of tests in just a second. First, though, we'll need to install the Chronic library for time parsing. That way, our test scripts can describe parties informally as starting at times like "Saturday at 10 p.m."

```
$ sudo gem install chronic
```

You can see Chronic in action at ❷ in the following code:

`story/novite_stories.rb`

```ruby
steps_for :planning do
  Given 'a party called "$name"' do |name|
    @party = Party.new(listener.browser)
    @party.name = name
  end

  Given 'a description of "$desc"' do |desc|
    @party.description = desc
  end
```

```
      Given 'a location of "$loc"' do |loc|
        @party.location = loc
      end

❶     Given /an? $event time of $sometime/ do |event, sometime|
        clean = sometime.gsub ',', ' '
❷       date_time = Chronic.parse clean, :now => Time.now - 86400

        if event == 'starting'
          @party.begins_at = date_time
        else
          @party.ends_at = date_time
        end
      end

      When 'I view the invitation' do
        @party.save_and_view
      end
    end
```

As we discussed earlier, step definitions can take regular expressions. At ❶, we've used one to match both "a starting" and "an ending."

Here are the steps for looking at an invitation after we've saved it:

story/novite_stories.rb

```
steps_for :reviewing do
  Then 'the $setting should be "$value"' do |setting, value|
    @party.send(setting).should == value
  end

  Then 'the party should $event on $date_time' do |event, date_time|
    actual_time =
      (event == 'begin') ?
      @party.begins_at :
      @party.ends_at

    clean = date_time.gsub ',', ' '
    expected_time = Chronic.parse clean, :now => Time.now - 86400

    actual_time.should == expected_time
  end

  Then 'I should see the Web address to send to my friends' do
    @party.link.should match(%r{^http://})
  end
end
```

Finally, we'll run the story:

`story/novite_stories.rb`

```ruby
with_steps_for :planning, :reviewing do
  run 'invite.story'
end
```

Now that we've written the top-level test script in plain text and the step definitions to mediate between plain text and Ruby, it's time to wade into the depths of the Selenium code to control the browser.

The Problem Domain

Let's take a first cut at that Party class. Now, before we get too carried away and add a bunch of nearly identical methods that look like this...

```ruby
def name
  @browser.get_text 'id=party_name'
end

def has_name?
  name rescue nil
end

def name=(name)
  @browser.type 'id=party_name', name
end

# repeat for location, description, etc.
```

Let's let Ruby write those methods for us:

`story/party.rb`

```ruby
require 'rubygems'
require 'selenium'
require 'time'

class Party
  def initialize(browser)
    @browser = browser
    @browser.open '/parties/new'
  end

  def self.def_setting(setting, type = :read_write)
    if type == :readable || type == :read_write
      define_method(setting) do
        @browser.get_text("id=party_#{setting}")
      end
```

```
      define_method("has_#{setting}?") do
        send(setting) rescue nil
      end
    end

    if type == :writable || type == :read_write
      define_method("#{setting}=") do |value|
        @browser.type "id=party_#{setting}", value
      end
    end
  end

  def_setting :name
  def_setting :description
  def_setting :location
  def_setting :link, :readable
  def_setting :notice, :readable
  def_setting :recipients, :writable
end
```

Setting the time is another operation that we can make simpler with a little finesse. The procedure is nearly identical for the starting and stopping times. We just need to select the year, month, day, hour, and minute, which are all combo boxes with IDs like party_begins_at_1i, party_begins_at_2i, and so on:

`story/party.rb`

```
class Party
  def begins_at=(time); set_time(:begin, time) end
  def ends_at=  (time); set_time(:end, time) end

  def set_time(event, time)
    ['%Y', '%B', '%d', '%H', '%M'].each_with_index do |part, index|
      element = "id=party_#{event}s_at_#{index + 1}i"
      value = time.strftime part

      @browser.select element, value
    end
  end
end
```

Retrieving the time is simpler. The web page for the invitation will describe the party like so: "You're invited to Celebration on Wednesday, September 29, 2010, from 12:30 PM to 12:35 PM!" We just have to pick out the starting time and do a little time math to figure out whether it ends on the same day or the next day.[2]

---

2. This code doesn't account for parties longer than twenty-four hours. We might want

```
story/party.rb
class Party
  def begins_at; get_times.first end
  def ends_at; get_times.last end

  def get_times
    begins_on = @browser.get_text 'party_begins_on'
    begins_at = @browser.get_text 'party_begins_at'
    ends_at = @browser.get_text 'party_ends_at'

    begins = Time.parse(begins_on + ' ' + begins_at)
    ends = Time.parse(begins_on + ' ' + ends_at)
    ends += 86400 if ends < begins

    [begins, ends]
  end

  def has_times?
    get_times rescue nil
  end
end
```

After all those gymnastics, the save_and_view() method is refreshingly straightforward:

```
story/party.rb
class Party
  def save_and_view
    @browser.click 'id=party_submit'
    @browser.wait_for_page_to_load 5000
    @saved = true
  end
end
```

Take what you have so far for a spin:

```
$ ruby novite_stories.rb
```

You should see something like Figure 10.1, on the following page. Now that we have a passing test, it's time to move on to the next story.

10.3 Extending Our Design

In the most basic and paranoid scenario, we don't want the party host to have to trust us with *any* email addresses: not his and not his

---

to allow this and reword the invitations or show an error message chiding the user's hard-partying habits. Feel free to add this use case as another story and update the app, if you like.

Figure 10.1: Partying with Selenium

guests'. We'll just hand him a chunk of text (including a link) he can paste into his email client and send out himself.

Once we've proven our trustworthiness, a few party planners may feel confident enough to let us send the email for them. These will contain simple "Yes" and "No" links right there in the message for the users to RSVP. Both these scenarios will be part of the RSVP story:

`story/rsvp.story`

```
Story: minimalist RSVPs
  As a guest with lots to do
  I want to RSVP to an invite with a minimum of mouse clicks
  So that I can get on with the rest of my tasks
```

Now, on to the scenarios.

RSVPing in a Web Form

First, we will look at the case where attendees RSVP manually on the web page.

```
story/rsvp.story
```

```
Scenario: email-free RSVPs
  Given a party called "a disco anniversary"
  When I view the invitation
  Then I should see the party details

  When I answer that "Robert Bell" will not attend
  Then I should see "Robert Bell" in the list of decliners
```

Novite contains an RSVP form right there on the party's own web page. There's no verification here. What happens if one of the host's friends starts maliciously RSVPing on behalf of other guests? Those sorts of people will stop getting invited to parties, that's what!

Our new version of the app looks like Figure 10.2, on the next page. Here's the latest batch of step definitions:

```
story/novite_stories.rb
```

```ruby
steps_for :rsvp do
  Then 'I should see the party details' do
    @party.should have_name
    @party.should have_description
    @party.should have_location
    @party.should have_times
  end

  When /I answer that "$guest" will( not)? attend/ do |guest, answer|
    attending = !answer.include?('not')
    @party.rsvp guest, attending
  end

  Then 'I should see "$guest" in the list of $type' do |guest, type|
    want_attending = (type == 'partygoers')
    @party.responses(want_attending).should include(guest)
  end
end
```

RSVPing is as simple as typing in a name, checking or unchecking the "attending" check box, and clicking the submit button:

```
story/party.rb
```

```ruby
class Party
  def rsvp(name, attending)
    @browser.type 'guest_name', name
    @browser.click 'guest_attending' unless attending
    @browser.click 'rsvp'
    @browser.wait_for_page_to_load 5000
  end
end
```

Figure 10.2: Invitation with RSVPs

Novite shows one big list of every guest who has RSVPed, right there on the invitation. So, all we have to do to figure out who's going to the party is use the XPath techniques from the previous chapter to loop through the list and then weed out the ones that do (or don't) have the word *not* in the appropriate place:

story/party.rb

```ruby
class Party
  RsvpItem = '//ul[@id="guests"]/li'

  def responses(want_attending)
    num_guests = @browser.get_xpath_count(RsvpItem).to_i
    return [] unless num_guests >= 1

    all = (1..num_guests).map do |i|
      name = @browser.get_text \
        "#{RsvpItem}[#{i}]/span[@class='rsvp_name']"
      rsvp = @browser.get_text \
        "#{RsvpItem}[#{i}]/span[@class='rsvp_attending']"
      [name, rsvp]
    end
```

```
    matching = all.select do |name, rsvp|
      is_attending = !rsvp.include?('not')
      !(want_attending ∧ is_attending)
    end

    matching.map {|name, rsvp| name}
  end
end
```

That takes care of using the web form. It's time to turn our attention to email.

RSVPing with a Link

We want our guests to be able to RSVP directly from an email message. First, we need to think about how the host is going to specify the recipients. Novite has an optional field where the host can type in a list of addresses separated by commas. So, we'll pop a couple of names into the list, parse the resulting email, and follow an RSVP link:

```
Scenario: RSVP links from email
  Given a party called "a salute to e-mail"
  And a guest list of "one@example.com,two@example.com"
  When I view the invitation
  Then I should see that e-mail was sent to "one@example.com,two@example.com"

  When I view the e-mail that was sent to "one@example.com"
  Then I should see "Yes/No" links
  When I follow the "Yes" link
  Then I should see "one@example.com" in the list of partygoers
```

In the real world, we'd probably do some kind of verification that the sender is not a spambot and then actually send the mail to a test server that we control. This version of Novite just pretends to send the message, so we'll have to fudge a little:

```
steps_for :email do
  Given 'a guest list of "$list"' do |list|
    @party.recipients = list
  end

  Then 'I should see that e-mail was sent to "$list"' do |list|
    @party.notice.include?(list).should be_true
  end

  When 'I view the e-mail that was sent to "$address"' do |address|
    @email = @party.email_to address
  end
```

```
Then 'I should see "Yes/No" links' do
  @email.should match(%r{Yes - http://})
  @email.should match(%r{No - http://})
end

When 'I follow the "$answer" link' do |answer|
  link = %r{#{answer} - (http://.+)}.match(@email)[1]
  @party.rsvp_at link
end
end
```

I've given Novite a special URL to show the email that *would* get sent to a particular party guest. The simplest way to implement this was to add a suffix to the normal URL for a party, as in http://party.txt?email=name%40example.com.

`story/party.rb`
```
class Party
  def email_to(address)
    @browser.open link + '.txt?email=' + address
    @browser.get_body_text
  end

  def rsvp_at(rsvp_link)
    @browser.open rsvp_link
  end
end
```

Now all that's left is to tell Story Runner to run our two new scenarios:

`story/novite_stories.rb`
```
with_steps_for :planning, :reviewing, :rsvp, :email do
  run 'rsvp.story'
end
```

Add that to the end of your step definition file and give it another whirl. You should see a whirlwind of web interaction, followed by a successful test report.

10.4 Where to Go from Here

This sure was a lot of code just to exercise the most simplistic of web apps. Fortunately, we're over the biggest hurdles. Adding new scenarios and stories will be much simpler, since the infrastructure is in place.

Was it worth it? I think so. Writing those stories forced a confrontation of every little nuance of the user interaction: what degree of privacy to offer, how exactly guests will RSVP to an invitation, and so forth. If you craft your tests in plain text, you stand a chance at being able to use them to communicate with the people who really matter: the ones who are going to be using your app.

Even so, take note of the effort required to write and maintain these test scripts. Automation is not a cheap prospect, and you'll need to consider the trade-offs in the context of your own project.

Whew! After a chapter this heavy, how about something a little lighter to finish off?

One More Thing:
Testing on the Mac

This final chapter will be a little breezier than the previous material. We're going to look at a few basic techniques for scripting OS X applications. But we're not going to delve too deeply into all the little gotchas and corner cases that we explored in the first half of this book with Windows and Swing programs.

We're actually going to do the opposite. We're going to find the minimum amount of effort it takes to port a couple of our existing text-editing tests to the TextEdit program that comes with Macs. If you're testing Mac apps, these ideas will just be a jumping-off point for your own explorations.

11.1 Taking the Reins

We're going to be using AppleScript to control an application's GUI. Many programs expose their own AppleScript interfaces, and if you're writing things like stress tests for Mac apps, you should definitely be using any scripting hooks your program provides.

This chapter will use something a little more universal, though: Apple's accessibility frameworks. This built-in feature of recent versions of OS X lets you send keystrokes and menu commands to nearly any program.[1] It still uses AppleScript, but instead of talking directly to the app, you talk to the System Events interface instead.

---

1. http://apple.com/applescript/uiscripting

To use this technique on your Mac, you'll need to turn on the accessibility features first. The setting is called "Enable access for assistive devices," and you'll find it in the System Preferences under Universal Access, as in Figure 11.1, on the facing page.

Here's a tiny script to copy and paste some text using the system text editor:

`one_more_thing/textedit.applescript`

```
tell application "TextEdit"
  activate
end tell

tell application "System Events"
  tell process "TextEdit"
    keystroke "H"
    keystroke "i"
  end tell
end tell

tell application "System Events"
  tell process "TextEdit"
    tell menu bar 1
      tell menu bar item "Edit"
        tell menu "Edit"
          click menu item "Select All"
          click menu item "Copy"
          set rightArrow to 124
          key code rightArrow
          click menu item "Paste"
        end tell
      end tell
    end tell
  end tell
end tell
```

You can run it directly from a Terminal window with the osascript command:

```
$ osascript textedit.applescript
```

AppleScript is lovely and all, but wouldn't it be nice if our Ruby test scripts looked like...well, Ruby? There are a couple of libraries that will do this for us, and we'll look at one of them in a moment. Most of these depend on some binary extensions to Ruby, though. It's worth putting together a rudimentary solution in pure Ruby first, just to see what's involved.

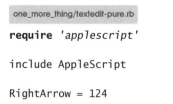

Figure 11.1: ENABLING GUI SCRIPTING

11.2 From AppleScript to Ruby

What we'd eventually like is to write test code that has the same verbs
as AppleScript but is recognizable as Ruby. For our TextEdit example,
we'd like something like this:

`one_more_thing/textedit-pure.rb`

```ruby
require 'applescript'

include AppleScript

RightArrow = 124
```

```
❶  tell.application("TextEdit").activate!

   tell.application("System Events").
     process("TextEdit").
     menu_bar(1).
❷    menu_bar_item("Edit").
❸    menu("Edit") do
       keystroke! "H"
       keystroke! "i"
       click_menu_item! "Select All"
       click_menu_item! "Copy"
       key_code! RightArrow
         click_menu_item! "Paste"
     end
```

For scripts this simple, we need only a few features in our AppleScript binding:

- A top-level tell() method like the one at ❶ will create a new scripting object to kick off a chain of AppleScript calls.

- Methods called on the scripting object become tell / end tell pairs in AppleScript (with underscores becoming spaces). So, ❷ will put a matching tell menu bar item "Edit" and end tell at the right places in the generated code.

- A Ruby method with an exclamation point, like the one at ❶, becomes just one line of AppleScript, with no tell or end tell. It should be the last method called in the chain, since it will (usually) cause the script to start running.

- Our test script can use a single Ruby block to group a few related commands together, as at ❸. Exclamation-point methods inside a block don't have an immediate effect; the block saves them up and runs the whole script as soon as it exits.

This is far from a universal Ruby-to-AppleScript translator. For one thing, it doesn't handle the using modifier in code like do something using something else. And it allows only single-parameter functions. But it's just enough to generate the AppleScript we need for these examples.

How do we get from application("TextEdit").activate! to tell application "TextEdit" / activate / end tell? We use that staple of Ruby metaprogramming, method_missing().

one_more_thing/applescript.rb

```
module AppleScript
  class Command
❶    def initialize
      @lines = []
      @tells = 0
    end

    def method_missing(name, *args, &block)
❷      immediate = name.to_s.include? '!'
      param = args.shift
      script = name.to_s.chomp('!').gsub('_', ' ')
      script += %Q( #{param.inspect}) if param

❸      unless immediate
        script = 'tell ' + script
        @tells += 1
      end

      @lines << script

❹      if block_given?
        @has_block = true
        instance_eval &block
        go!
      elsif immediate && !@has_block
        go!
      else
        self
      end
    end
  end
end
```

A more sophisticated approach would require us to do lots of bookkeeping with things like the levels of nesting. But the simple binding we're building doesn't need to worry about interleaving tell and non-tell commands. A simple array of commands and a count of how many end tells we need at the end are all we need to track at ❶.

At ❷, we do the basic string processing to build up a line of Apple-Script: detecting exclamation points, turning underscores to spaces, and putting quotes around string arguments.

At ❸, we track whether this is a single-line command to run immediately or a tell / end tell pair.

Finally, at ❹, we figure out whether we're looking at the last statement in the script, so we can make the decision to run everything now or just return the script object (so that the test script can chain a bunch of commands off each other).

The go!() method just needs to concatenate all the lines together and send them to AppleScript:

`one_more_thing/applescript.rb`

```
module AppleScript
  class Command
    def go!
      clauses = @lines.map do |line|
        '-e "' + line.gsub('"', '\"') + '"'
      end.join(' ') + ' '

      clauses += '-e "end tell" ' * @tells

      `osascript #{clauses}`.chomp("\n")
    end
  end
end
```

As we saw earlier, osascript runs AppleScript programs. Normally, you pass it a filename to read, but you can also just send it a chunk of script with the -e option. This option accepts only very short excerpts, but you can pass several -e arguments in a row.

The last piece is the module-level tell() method, which is trivial:

`one_more_thing/applescript.rb`

```
module AppleScript
  def tell
    Command.new
  end
end
```

With essentially a twenty-line method_missing() function, we've managed to put together a basic, but functional, AppleScript generator in Ruby. It'll handle the simple kinds of scripting calls where you just need to do a little typing and maybe activate a pull-down menu or two.

Now, this class won't handle more complicated actions. And there's definitely an overhead to launching an external osascript process for every GUI action. It's time to graduate to a more sophisticated library.

A Faster, Better Bridge

RubyOSA and rb-appscript, two popular Ruby/AppleScript bindings, remove the overhead of a separate process by interacting directly with

Apple's scripting APIs.[2,3] Both libraries have glue-code portions written in C. If you don't mind installing a binary gem, you can get faster, more flexible interoperability between the two languages than with the previous pure-Ruby approach.

For the simple tests in this chapter, either library would do just fine. For no particular reason other than that I find it slightly easier to use, I'll give examples using rb-appscript:

```
$ sudo gem install rb-appscript
```

Here's how the previous simple TextEdit automation steps translate to rb-appscript:

```
one_more_thing/textedit.rb
require 'rubygems'
require 'appscript'

include Appscript

app("TextEdit").activate

events = app("System Events")
events.keystroke "H"
events.keystroke "i"

edit = app('System Events').
  processes['TextEdit'].
  menu_bars[1].
  menu_bar_items['Edit'].
  menus['Edit']

edit.menu_items['Select All'].click
edit.menu_items['Copy'].click

RightArrow = 124
events.key_code RightArrow

edit.menu_items['Paste'].click
```

As you can see, it's pretty similar to our pure-Ruby wrapper. Collections such as menus are treated a little more like Ruby objects with rb-appscript. Rather than saying click_menu_item('Paste'), you fetch the entire menu_items collection, index it using square brackets, and then call the click() method.

11.3 RSpec and AppleScript

TextEdit is a general-purpose editing program. It does not have the encryption and password features of LockNote or JunqueNote. So, we're going to take the tests we developed in Chapter 5, *The Home Stretch*, on page 61 and narrow them down just to basic editor stuff: Cut, Copy, Paste, and Undo.

We're using almost exactly the same test script from the first half of this book—that's the whole point of the exercise. There is actually one difference as to how the various apps implement Undo, though. LockNote and JunqueNote undo character-by-character, while TextEdit can undo multiple characters at a time. Here's the new body of the Undo test:

```
one_more_thing/note_spec.rb
```

```ruby
@note.text = 'abc'
@note.text = 'def'

@note.undo
@note.text.should == 'abc'

@note.undo
@note.text.should be_empty
```

We're going to implement only a couple of the features of the Note class. But we can still use the same note.rb from before, as long as we leave those unused features alone. We just need to provide a new TextNote class for the AppleScript stuff. Here's the startup and shutdown code, using our pure-Ruby AppleScript generator:

```
one_more_thing/textnote.rb
```

```ruby
require 'applescript'
require 'note'

class TextNote < Note
  include AppleScript

  @@app = TextNote

  def initialize(name = 'Untitled', with_options = {})
    tell.application('TextEdit').activate!
  end

  DontSave = 2

  def exit!
    menu 'TextEdit', 'Quit TextEdit'
```

```
    tell.
      application('System Events').
      process('TextEdit').
      window('Untitled').
      sheet(1).
❶    click_button!(DontSave)
  end

  def running?
    tell.
      application('System Events').
❷    process!('TextEdit') == 'TextEdit'
  end
end
```

We won't bother to record whether a Save prompt appears, but we still need to watch for it and click the right button. The Don't Save button has a fancy UTF-8 apostrophe in it. Rather than deal with character encodings here, we'll just click the button by its order in the dialog box at ❶.

❷ is the first place where we've actually looked at the output of osascript. AppleScript will return either the string *TextEdit* or an error message. The latter will show up on stderr, too, so we'll need to deal with that when it's time to run the script. Setting and getting text is pretty similar to what we've done before:

`one_more_thing/textnote.rb`

```
class TextNote
  def text
    tell.
      application('System Events').
      process('TextEdit').
      window('Untitled').
      scroll_area(1).
      text_area(1).
      get_value!
  end

  def text=(new_text)
    select_all

    tell.application('System Events').
      process('TextEdit').
      window('Untitled') do
        new_text.split(//).each {|k| keystroke! k}
      end
  end
end
```

Menus are also straightforward:

one_more_thing/textnote.rb

```
class TextNote
  def menu(name, item, wait = false)
    tell.application('System Events').
      process('TextEdit').
      menu_bar(1).
      menu_bar_item(name).
      menu(name).
      click_menu_item! item
  end

❶ def undo; menu('Edit', 1) end

  def select_all; menu('Edit', 'Select All') end
  def cut; menu('Edit', 'Cut') end
  def copy; menu('Edit', 'Copy') end
  def paste; menu('Edit', 'Paste') end
end
```

The only thing to note is that the Undo menu item's caption changes while you're editing the document; it becomes Undo Typing, Undo Cut, or what have you. So at ❶, we have to invoke it by its relative position inside the Edit menu instead.

Believe it or not, that's all it takes to port these tests to the Mac. Give it a whirl, and feel free to redirect stderr somewhere to keep the AppleScript warnings out of the main test report:

```
$ spec -rtextnote -fs note_spec.rb 2>/dev/null
```

That should be enough to get a bit of the flavor of testing GUIs through AppleScript. For your own tests, there are a lot more factors to think about: internationalization, file dialog boxes, and so forth.

You may find it helpful to have an automated tool to help you browse through an application's interface and find the right nested set of "text area within a scroll area within a window" descriptions. Apple provides a decent free one called UI Element Inspector.[4] You can find paid alternatives as well.

So, there you have it—a whirlwind tour of GUI testing techniques. I hope you've enjoyed the ride and have also absorbed a little healthy skepticism toward automation along the way. Thanks for coming along; I can't wait to hear about the cool tests you'll build. Take care.

---

4. http://www.apple.com/applescript/uiscripting/downloads/uiinspector.dmg

Appendix A

Other Windows Techniques

The Windows examples in this book all used the Win32API Ruby library to control applications. Win32API was a good fit for the needs of these apps. It's mature, it ships with the Windows build of Ruby, and it's a simple base on which to build good testing abstractions.

Win32API is far from the only way to control a Windows program from Ruby, though. There are several other libraries and techniques that may be a good fit for your application.

A.1 Windows Script Host

For several years, Windows has shipped with the Windows Script Host library to help system administrators automate some of their routine tasks (http://msdn.microsoft.com/en-us/library/9bbdkx3k.aspx).

Like testers, admins often find themselves needing to drive an application that doesn't have its own developer API. Through the WshShell COM object, scripts can launch apps, search for windows by title, and send keystrokes. (Of course, they can also do lots of non-GUI things, such as interact with the file system, create COM objects, and so on.)

Here's a tiny snippet of WSH code so you can get a feel for the differences between it and the Win32 API:

windows/wsh.rb

```
require 'win32ole'

wsh = WIN32OLE.new 'Wscript.Shell'

wsh.Exec 'notepad'
sleep 1
```

```
wsh.AppActivate 'Untitled - Notepad'

wsh.SendKeys 'This is some text'

wsh.SendKeys '%EA'
wsh.SendKeys 'And this is its replacement'
wsh.SendKeys '%{F4}'

if wsh.AppActivate 'Notepad'
  wsh.SendKeys 'n'
end
```

As you can see, typing keystrokes into the app is considerably simpler. Instead of having to look up virtual key codes in a table and manually construct a sequence of key-down/key-up events, you can just pass SendKeys the characters you want to type. There's even a simple notation for key combinations (for example, %{F4} for Alt+F4).

On the downside, WSH doesn't really provide an easy way to get information back out of a program. For example, we can't read the text in a window or drill down into a dialog box to find out whether a button is enabled.

Fortunately, there's nothing preventing you from using the two APIs side by side in your test script. You could easily use WSH for launching apps and typing keystrokes and use the Windows API for the rest.

A.2 Win32::GuiTest

In 2002, a coder nicknamed "MoonWolf" ported the Win32::GuiTest library from Perl to Ruby (http://raa.ruby-lang.org/project/win32-guitest). At its heart, GuiTest is a catalog of commonly used Windows API function wrappers. So, rather than having to look up a ton of C functions in the MSDN documentation and write their Ruby versions yourself, you can just use the provided definitions.

Here's the same simple script as before, ported to GuiTest:

```
windows/wgui.rb
```

```
    require 'win32/guitest'
❶   require 'win32/guitest_svn'

    include Win32::GuiTest

    system 'start "" "C:/Windows/System32/notepad.exe"'
    sleep 1
```

```
w = findWindowLike(nil, /^Untitled - Notepad$/).first
w.sendkeys 'This is some text'
w.sendkeys ctrl('a')
w.sendkeys 'And this is its replacement'

e = w.children.find {|c| c.classname == 'Edit'}
puts e.windowText

w.sendkeys alt(key('F4'))
sleep 0.5

d = findWindowLike(nil, /^Notepad$/).first
d.sendkeys 'n'
```

❷ (marker next to `puts e.windowText`)

As you can see, this library can do the same sorts of things as WSH. But GuiTest can also pick apart the window structure and get text back from the app, as we've done at ❷.

To get the best use of the code, you'll need some updates that Wayne Vucenic and Chris McMahon gave the project in 2005.[1] Their repository on RubyForge contains both the original MoonWolf code and their new version. Each has features the other lacks. In a real project, you might combine the two, presumably a little more elegantly than just squishing them together the way I did at ❶ (and causing an avalanche of redefinition warnings).

GuiTest has some nice touches, such as the ability to use regular expressions to search for windows. And the API will be familiar to developers coming from the original Perl library. It wasn't a perfect match for the examples in this book because it's a bit tricky to install and because its Windows-like API didn't seem at home alongside more stereotypical Ruby code.

A.3   Winobj

Winobj aims to provide a more Ruby-like wrapper around the Windows API.[2] Rather than dumping all the Win32 functions into one flat namespace, Winobj provides separate classes for buttons, edit controls, labels, and so forth. When it first connects to a top-level window, it automatically finds the children of the window and creates Ruby objects to represent them.

---

1. http://rubyforge.org/projects/guitest
2. http://rubyforge.org/projects/wet-winobj

The following is the familiar Notepad exercise. I've omitted the step where we exit the app, because we'd have to supply our own custom window-closing code.

windows/wobj.rb

```ruby
require 'wet-winobj'
require 'winobjects/WinLabel'
require 'winobjects/WinCheckbox'
require 'winobjects/WinRadio'

include Wet::WinUtils
include Wet::Winobjects

system 'start "" "C:/Windows/System32/notepad.exe"'
sleep 1

w = app_window 'title' => 'Untitled - Notepad'

e = w.child_objects.first
e.set 'This is some text'
e.set 'And this is its replacement'
puts e.text
```

Winobj is more of an automation library than a testing library. Instead of simulating keystrokes to fill in a text window, it will just set the text directly by sending the process a message. As of this writing, the library provides only a few simple window operations, and some features take a lot of fiddling to get working. If you're just writing a quick stress test to try to overfill an edit control and crash a program, this basic level of control may be all you need.

A.4 A Few Win32 Definitions

These libraries may or may not be a perfect match for your project. I hope this book has demonstrated that you can roll your own abstractions atop Win32API fairly easily in Ruby. If you decide to go down that path, here are the constant definitions used in the first part of the book:

home_stretch/windows_gui.rb

```ruby
# Windows messages - general
WM_COMMAND = 0x0111
WM_SYSCOMMAND = 0x0112
SC_CLOSE = 0xF060

# Windows messages - text
WM_GETTEXT = 0x000D
EM_GETSEL = 0x00B0
EM_SETSEL = 0x00B1
```

```
# Commonly-used control IDs
IDOK = 1
IDCANCEL = 2
IDYES = 6
IDNO = 7

# Mouse and keyboard flags
MOUSEEVENTF_LEFTDOWN = 0x0002
MOUSEEVENTF_LEFTUP = 0x0004
KEYEVENTF_KEYDOWN = 0
KEYEVENTF_KEYUP = 2

# Modifier keys
VK_SHIFT = 0x10
VK_CONTROL = 0x11
VK_MENU = 0x12          # Alt

# Commonly-used keys
VK_BACK = 0x08
VK_TAB = 0x09
VK_RETURN = 0x0D
VK_ESCAPE = 0x1B
VK_OEM_1 = 0xBA         # semicolon (US)
VK_OEM_102 = 0xE2       # backslash (US)
VK_OEM_PERIOD = 0xBE
VK_HOME = 0x24
VK_END = 0x23
VK_OEM_COMMA = 0xBC
```

And here are the API calls we encountered:

home_stretch/windows_gui.rb

```
def_api 'FindWindow',          ['P', 'P'], 'L'
def_api 'FindWindowEx',        ['L', 'L', 'P', 'P'], 'L'
def_api 'SendMessage',         ['L', 'L', 'L', 'P'], 'L', :send_with_buffer
def_api 'SendMessage',         ['L', 'L', 'L', 'L'], 'L'
def_api 'PostMessage',         ['L', 'L', 'L', 'L'], 'L'
def_api 'keybd_event',         ['I', 'I', 'L', 'L'], 'V'
def_api 'GetDlgItem',          ['L', 'L'], 'L'
def_api 'GetWindowRect',       ['L', 'P'], 'I'
def_api 'SetCursorPos',        ['L', 'L'], 'I'
def_api 'mouse_event',         ['L', 'L', 'L', 'L', 'L'], 'V'
def_api 'IsWindow',            ['L'], 'L'
def_api 'IsWindowVisible',     ['L'], 'L'
def_api 'SetForegroundWindow', ['L'], 'L'
```

As you can see, this is only the barest of lists. You'll probably need to add a couple more constants and function calls from the official API documentation.[3] But even the few items shown here will get you started toward building your own library for scripting Windows apps.

---

3.   http://msdn.microsoft.com/en-us/library/aa383749.aspx

Appendix B

Resources

B.1 Websites

RSpec . . . . http://rspec.info
RSpec's headquarters contains full API documentation, downloads, plenty of examples, and links to its creators' BDD articles.

Behaviour-Driven Development . . . . http://behaviour-driven.org
This wiki maintained by Dan North has tons of BDD articles and links.

Ruby on Windows . . . . http://rubyonwindows.blogspot.com
David Mullet's blog offers tons of practical techniques for controlling Windows applications from Ruby.

"Architectures of Test Automation" . . . . . http://www.kaner.com/testarch.html
Actually, you should read everything on Cem Kaner's website, but this article in particular summarizes tons of research on test automation.

James Bach . . . . http://www.satisfice.com/blog
James's writing will urge you to confront exactly what information your tests are supposed to reveal and then challenge you to design them accordingly.

Brian Marick . . . . http://www.exampler.com
Brian covers test construction, automation trade-offs, and programmer/tester roles, all under the umbrella of exploratory testing.

B.2 Books

Lessons Learned in Software Testing [CK02]
> These guys have seen it all when it comes to testing, GUI or otherwise. Before you set off tilting at the windmill of 100% automation, read what this book has to say about the right time and place for automated testing.

Facts and Fallacies of Software Engineering [Gla92]
Robert Glass has been gathering data for decades and has seen which software practices work and which do not, including the thorny issues of testing and tools.

Everyday Scripting with Ruby [Mar06]
Brian writes about the nuts and bolts of the using the language—getting Ruby, how to structure and run your programs, and so on—to solve real-life problems.

B.3 Bibliography

[CK02]   Bret Pettichord Cem Kaner, James Bach. *Lessons Learned in Software Testing: A Context-Driven Approach.* John Wiley & Sons, New York, 2002.

[Gla92]   Robert L. Glass. *Facts and Fallacies of Software Engineering.* Addison-Wesley Professional, Reading, MA, 1992.

[Het84]   William C. Hetzel. *The Complete Guide to Software Testing.* QED Information Sciences, Wellesley, MA, 1984.

[Mar06]   Brian Marick. *Everyday Scripting with Ruby: For Teams, Testers, and You.* The Pragmatic Programmers, LLC, Raleigh, NC, and Dallas, TX, 2006.

[Mye79]   Glenford J. Myers. *The Art of Software Testing.* John Wiley & Sons, New York, 1979.

Index

It All Starts Here

If you're programming in Ruby, you need the PickAxe Book: the definitive reference to the Ruby Programming language, now in the revised 3rd Edition for Ruby 1.9. Or check out how to use FXRuby, a popular, cross-platform GUI.

Programming Ruby (The Pickaxe)

The Pickaxe book, named for the tool on the cover, is the definitive reference to this highly-regarded language. • Up-to-date and expanded for Ruby version 1.9 • Complete documentation of all the built-in classes, modules, and methods • Complete descriptions of all standard libraries • Learn more about Ruby's web tools, unit testing, and programming philosophy

Programming Ruby: The Pragmatic Programmer's Guide, 3rd Edition
Dave Thomas with Chad Fowler and Andy Hunt
(900 pages) ISBN: 978-1-9343560-8-1. $49.95
http://pragprog.com/titles/ruby3

FXRuby

Get started developing GUI applications using FXRuby. With a combination of tutorial exercises and focused, technical information, this book goes beyond the basics to equip you with proven, practical knowledge and techniques for developing real-world FXRuby applications. Learn directly from the lead developer of FXRuby, and you'll be writing powerful and sophisticated GUIs in your favorite programming language.

FXRuby Create Lean and Mean GUIs with Ruby
Lyle Johnson
(240 pages) ISBN: 978-1-9343560-7-4. $36.95
http://pragprog.com/titles/fxruby

Web 2.0

Welcome to the Web, version 2.0. You need some help to tame the wild technologies out there. Start with Prototype and script.aculo.us, a book about two libraries that will make your JavaScript life much easier. See how to reach the largest possible web audience with The Accessible Web.

Prototype and script.aculo.us

Tired of getting swamped in the nitty-gritty of cross-browser, Web 2.0–grade JavaScript? Get back in the game with Prototype and script.aculo.us, two extremely popular JavaScript libraries that make it a walk in the park. Be it Ajax, drag and drop, autocompletion, advanced visual effects, or many other great features, all you need is write one or two lines of script that look so good they could almost pass for Ruby code!

Prototype and script.aculo.us: You never knew JavaScript could do this!
Christophe Porteneuve
(330 pages) ISBN: 1-934356-01-8. $34.95
http://pragprog.com/titles/cppsu

The Accessible Web

The 2000 U.S. Census revealed that 12% of the population is severely disabled. Sometime in the next two decades, one in five Americans will be older than 65. Section 508 of the Americans with Disabilities Act requires your website to provide *equivalent access* to all potential users. But beyond the law, it is both good manners and good business to make your site accessible to everyone. This book shows you how to design sites that excel for all audiences.

The Accessible Web
Jeremy Sydik
(304 pages) ISBN: 1-934356-02-6. $34.95
http://pragprog.com/titles/jsaccess

The Pragmatic Bookshelf

The Pragmatic Bookshelf features books written by developers for developers. The titles continue the well-known Pragmatic Programmer style and continue to garner awards and rave reviews. As development gets more and more difficult, the Pragmatic Programmers will be there with more titles and products to help you stay on top of your game.

Visit Us Online

Scripted GUI Testing with Ruby's Home Page
http://pragprog.com/titles/idgtr
Source code from this book, errata, and other resources. Come give us feedback, too!

Register for Updates
http://pragprog.com/updates
Be notified when updates and new books become available.

Join the Community
http://pragprog.com/community
Read our weblogs, join our online discussions, participate in our mailing list, interact with our wiki, and benefit from the experience of other Pragmatic Programmers.

New and Noteworthy
http://pragprog.com/news
Check out the latest pragmatic developments in the news.

Save on the PDF

Save on the PDF version of this book. Owning the paper version of this book entitles you to purchase the PDF version at a terrific discount. The PDF is great for carrying around on your laptop. It's hyperlinked, has color, and is fully searchable.

Buy it now at pragprog.com/coupon.

Contact Us

Phone Orders:	1-800-699-PROG (+1 919 847 3884)
Online Orders:	www.pragprog.com/catalog
Customer Service:	orders@pragprog.com
Non-English Versions:	translations@pragprog.com
Pragmatic Teaching:	academic@pragprog.com
Author Proposals:	proposals@pragprog.com